Poldi Zeitlin
David Goldberg

Understanding Music Theory

Thorough
A full introduction to music theory
Logical
Introduces new concepts step-by-step
Practical
A worksheet with every lesson to let you monitor your own progress
Enjoyable
Makes learning fun with easy-to-understand explanations and examples

OMNIBUS PRESS

Exclusive Distributors:
Book Sales Limited
8/9 Frith Street, London W1D 3JB
Music Sales Corporation
257 Park Avenue South,
New York, NY10010, USA
Music Sales Pty. Limited
120 Rothschild Avenue, Rosebery, NSW 2018, Australia.

To the Music Trade only:
Music Sales Limited, 8/9 Frith Street, London W1D 3JB

Copyright © 1986, 2001 Omnibus Press
(A Division of Book Sales Ltd)

All rights reserved. No part of this book may be reproduced in any form
or by an electronic or mechanical means, including information storage
or retrieval systems, without permission in writing from the publisher,
except by a reviewer who may quote brief passages.

CONTENTS

Each lesson is backed up with a work sheet

PART ONE

LESSONS

1. The Musical Alphabet and Keyboard, 5
2. Some Notes and Their Time Values, 7
3. Time Signatures and Bars, 9
4. Understanding Notation, 11
5. The Grand Stave, 13
6. Rests, 15
7. Some New Notes, 17
8. Sharps, 19
9. Flats, 21
10. Quavers, 23
11. Curved Lines and Dots, 25
12. Some More Signs and Italian Words, 27
13. More New Notes, 29
14. Upbeats, 31
15. Review Work Sheet, 33

PART TWO

LESSONS

1. Tones and Semitones, 35
2. Ledger Lines, 37
3. Scales, 39
4. Scale Degrees and Tetrachords, 41
5. Writing the Major Scale, 43
6. Dotted Crotchet, 45
7. Intervals, 47
8. Six Eight Time, 49
9. Key Signatures, 51
10. Major Triads, 53
11. Some More Intervals, 55
12. Semiquavers, 57
13. Tonic and Dominant, 59
14. Harmonising Melodies, 61
15. Review Work Sheet, 63

PART THREE

LESSONS
1 A Review of Intervals. Minor Thirds, 65
2 Minor Triads, 67
3 Harmonising Melodies using Minor Triads, 69
4 Minor Scales and the Minor Scale Outline, 71
5 The Ascending Melodic Minor Scale, 73
6 Natural Minor Scales and Minor Key Signatures, 75
7 Piano-Style Accompaniments, 77
8 Harmonising Minor Key Melodies, 79
9 The Harmonic Minor Scale, 81
10 Triplets, 83
11 Exact names of all Major, Minor and Perfect Intervals, 85
12 The Dominant Seventh Chord, 87
13 Using the Dominant Seventh Chord, 89
14 Summary of Minor Scales and Triads, 91
15 Review Work Sheet, 93

ANSWERS

Part One, 97
Part Two, 105
Part Three, 113

PART ONE
LESSON 1
THE MUSICAL ALPHABET AND THE KEYBOARD

There are just seven letters in the musical alphabet: A B C D E F G. Can you say them backwards?

The lowest key on the left of the Piano Keyboard is A. After that, the white keys are named B C D E F and G. Then we start again with A.

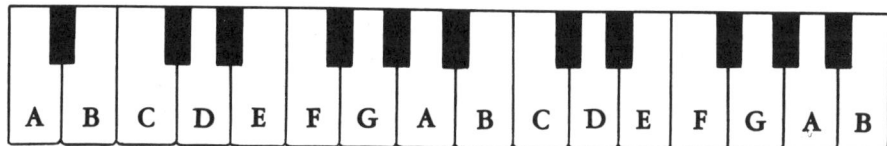

The white keys touch each other, but the black keys are arranged in groups of twos and threes. Find all the groups of two black keys. Next find all the groups of three black keys. Can you do this without looking? The white key between the two black keys is D. How many D's can you find?

What is the name of the key to the left of D? The key to the right? Play all the C D E's. G and A are the white keys between the three black keys. Play all the G A's on your piano.

What is the name of the key to the left of G? The one to the right of A? Play all the F G A B's. You know the names of all the white keys on the piano.

WORK SHEET 1

1. Put a circle ◯ around all the groups of two black keys on this keyboard.

2. Put a box ▢ around all the groups of three black keys on this keyboard.

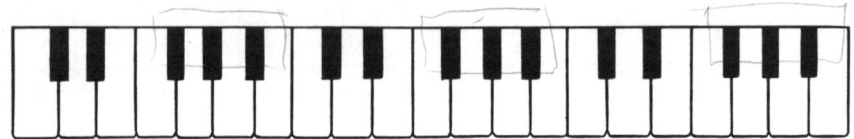

3. Write the musical alphabet starting on E.   E F G A B C D
4. Write the musical alphabet backwards starting on G.   G F E D C B A
5. Write the letters which come before and after the following letters in the musical alphabet.
   A B C   D E F   B C D   F G A   E F G   G A B   C D E
6. Mark all the D's and G's on this keyboard.

7. Write in the names of all the keys which are marked on this keyboard.

LESSON 2
SOME NOTES AND THEIR TIME VALUES

In listening to music and singing, you have probably noticed that some notes last longer than others. In writing music we show this by making different kinds of notes.

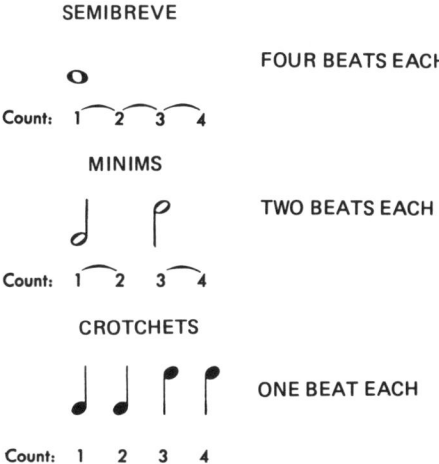

Just as an apple can be cut into two halves or four quarters, a semi-breve can be divided into two minims or four crotchets.

If we place a dot after a minim, it will get three beats — two for the note and one for the dot. This is called a DOTTED MINIM.

A DOT PLACED AFTER A NOTE ALWAYS GETS HALF AS MANY BEATS AS THE NOTE ITSELF

What kind of notes are these? How many beats does each one get?

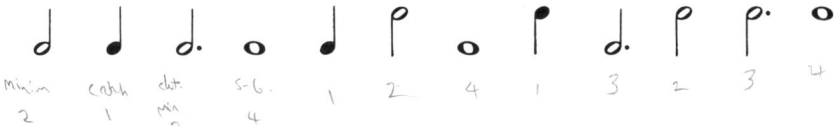

The stem of a note may go either up or down. But stems always go up on the right side. If the stem goes down, it is placed on the left side of the note.

WORK SHEET 2

1. Draw: A Minim   A Crotchet   A Semibreve   A Dotted Minim

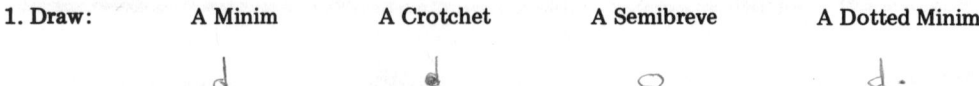

(Be sure the stems are on the correct side!)

2. How many beats does each of these notes get?

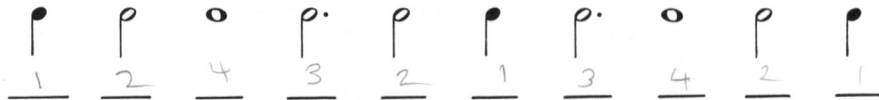

    1   2   4   3   2   1   3   4   2   1

3. Write the note or notes which get the same number of beats as the ones given here.

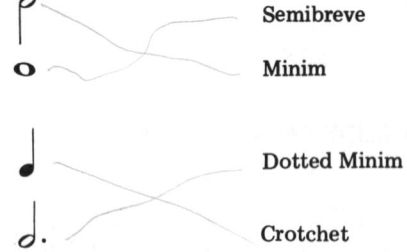

4. Draw a line to connect the things which match.

Semibreve

Minim

Dotted Minim

Crotchet

5. Circle the groups of two black keys and mark F G A B. Be careful!

LESSON 3
TIME SIGNATURES AND BARS

In music, a *Bar* is the distance between two bar lines.

The most common *Time Signatures* are 2/4, 3/4, and 4/4. The top number always tells us how many beats there are in a bar. The bottom number tells us what kind of note gets one beat.

        2/4   Two beats in a bar
                      A crotchet gets one beat

        3/4   Three beats in a bar
                      A crotchet gets one beat

        4/4   Four beats in a bar
                      A crotchet gets one beat

Here are some examples with the beats written in. See if you can clap them while counting out loud.

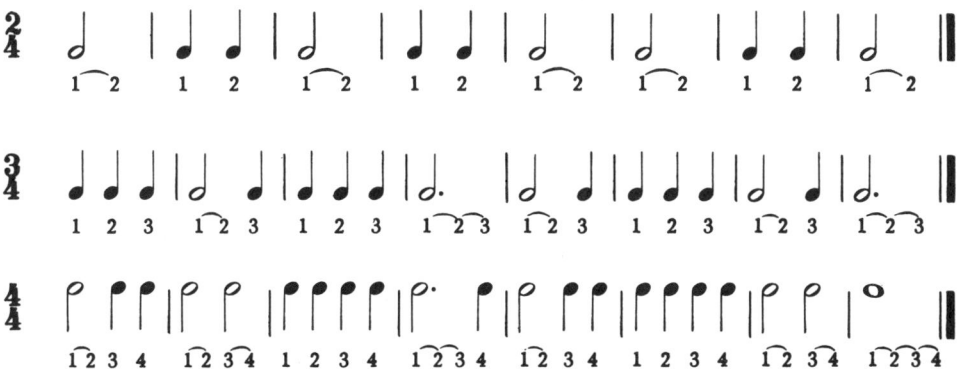

Notice that we always put a vertical line | called a *Bar Line* before the note which will receive the first count in the bar. At the end of the piece we put a *Double Bar*. ‖

WORK SHEET 3

1. Write in the beats for these examples.

2. Correct the bars which do not have the right number of beats by adding extra notes or by crossing out others.

3. The Time Signatures have been left out. Put in the right ones.

LESSON 4
UNDERSTANDING NOTATION

If we draw a line and call it G, any note which that line goes through will be named G. If we place a note above the line, it will be the note above G, that is, A. What is the name of the note below the line? Here is a tune with three notes.

If we add another line above this line, it will be the next note after A. Just remember that each line is a note and the space between the lines is a note. They go up in alphabetical order and we play keys one after another on the keyboard.

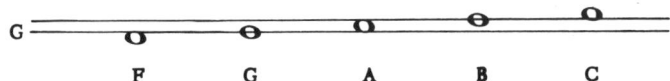

If we go from one line to the next, we skip one letter-name for the space and must also skip one key on the keyboard. The same is true if we go from one space to another—we skip the line.

In this next example can you tell which notes are moving in steps and which are skips?

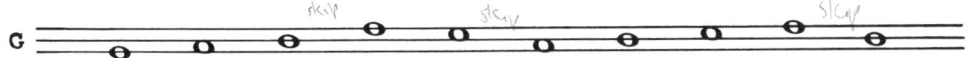

So far we have written music on one, two or three lines. But printed music is always written on five lines called a *Stave*. Just remember that each line and each space represents a note.

WORK SHEET 4

1. Write in the names of the following notes.

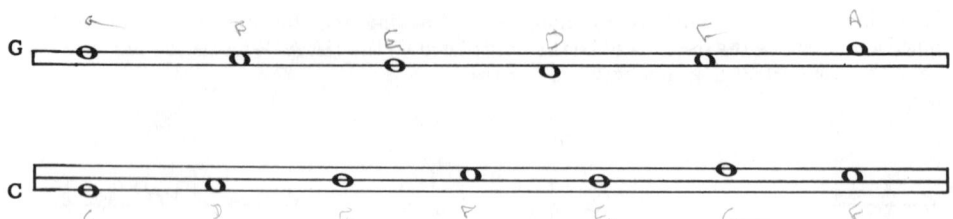

2. Draw an arrow to show whether the notes are moving up ↗, remaining the same →, or going down ↘

3. Circle the skips and mark S for the steps.

4. Write in the names of the keys marked on the keyboard.

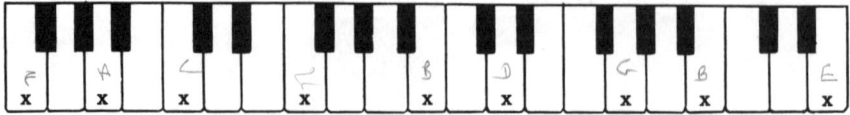

5. Write in the counting for the following bars.

LESSON 5
THE GRAND STAVE

All we must do to work out the names of all the lines and spaces on the five line stave is to give one line a name. Many years ago people simply put a G on the second line as we did in the last lesson. That G got fancier and fancier until we now make it like this:

G *Clef*

Remember that it is still a G and is on the second line. It is a *G Clef*.

In writing piano music we also use another clef sign. It is called *F Clef* because it tells us that the fourth line is F. It is interesting to see how this clef grew out of the letter F.

F *Clef*

Practise making G clefs and F clefs until you can make them like the ones given here.

When we write music for the piano we put the G clef on one stave and the F clef on another and connect the two with a *Brace*. This is called a *Grand Stave*.

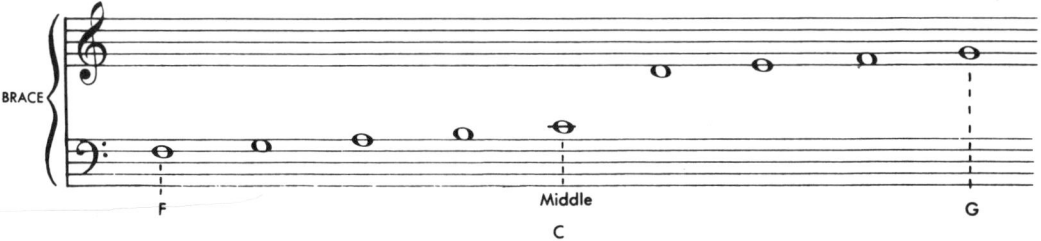

There is another line between the two staves of the grand stave. It is *Middle C* and tells us to play the C nearest to the centre of the keyboard. We put it in only when we want to write C. We now have three *Guide Posts* on the grand stave. The centre line is *Middle C*. The G clef tells us that the second line of that stave is the G above middle C. The F clef tells us that the fourth line of that stave is the F below middle C. Since we know the alphabet very well now, it is easy to work out the names of all the notes in between the *Guide Posts*.

WORK SHEET 5

1. Draw three *G Clefs*.   Draw three *F Clefs*.

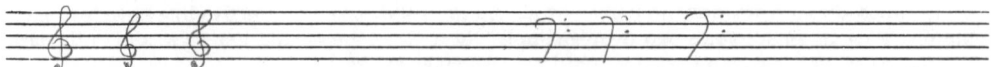

2. Write the note above each of the notes written on the *Grand Stave*.

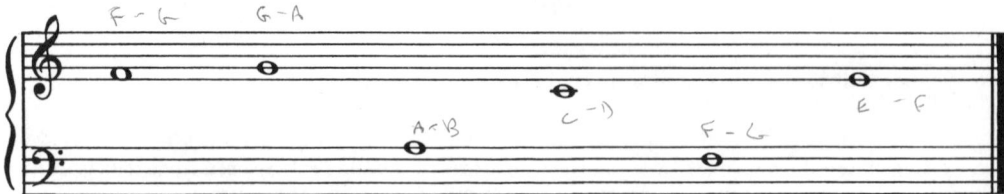

3. Write the note below each of the notes written on the *Grand Stave*.

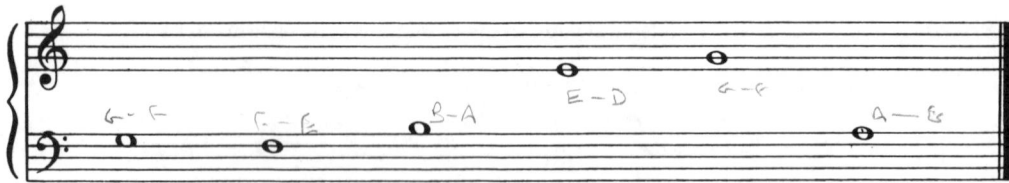

4. Write the names of these notes.

5. Write in the beats of these bars.

LESSON 6
RESTS

You have already learned about semibreves, minims and crotchets. In music we also have signs for silence. These are called *Rests*. Just like the notes, we have *Semibreve, Minim* and *Crotchet Rests*. The *Semibreve Rest* and the *Minim Rest* look very much alike. The only difference is that the *Semibreve Rest* hangs from the fourth line while the *Minim Rest* sits on the third line.

The *Semibreve Rest* is also used for a whole bar even if there are not four beats in the measure. There are two different ways of making the *Crotchet Rest*. When it is printed in music it usually looks like the one on the left. But when made by hand, it usually looks like the one on the right. Try to make some of the second type.

Can you identify these rests? How many beats does each one get?

Write in the beats and then clap the following examples.

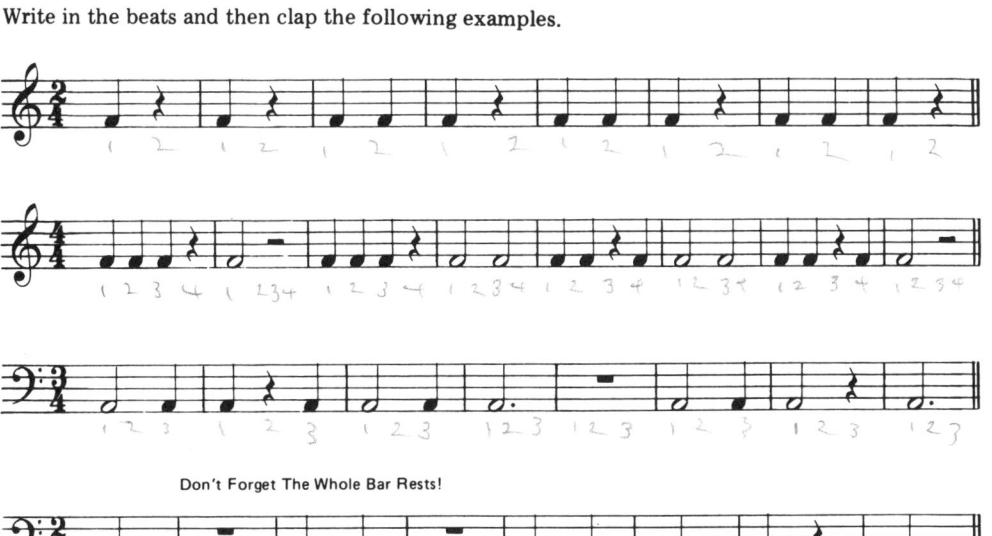

Don't Forget The Whole Bar Rests!

WORK SHEET 6

1. Draw a rest which gets the same number of beats as each of these notes.

2. Write in the number of beats each of these rests or notes should get in $\frac{4}{4}$ time.

3. Complete the following bars by adding one note.

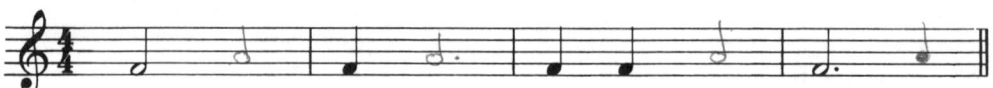

4. Complete these bars by adding one rest.

5. The names of the notes in each of these bars spell a word. See if you can work out what they spell.

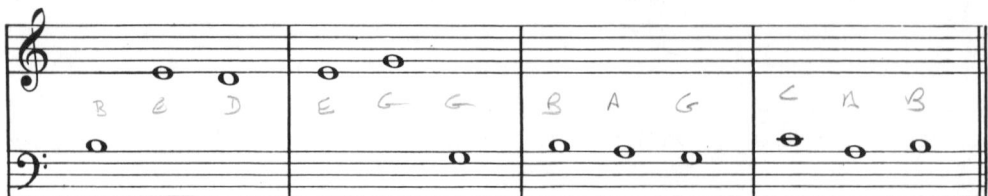

LESSON 7
SOME NEW NOTES

Here are some new notes. If you remember that the lines and spaces are in alphabetical order you can very easily work out the names of the three notes below our Guide Post F and the three notes above our Guide Post G.

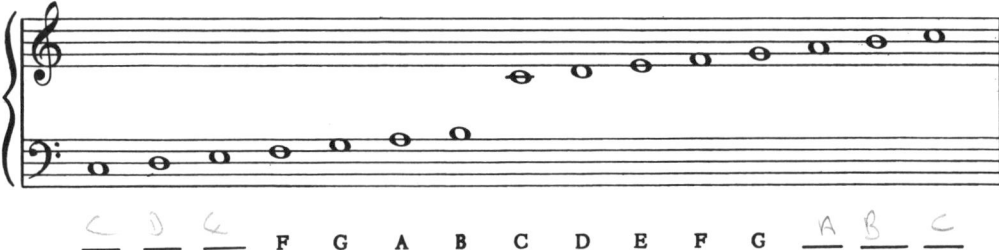

<u>C</u> <u>D</u> <u>E</u>   F   G   A   B   C   D   E   F   G   <u>A</u> <u>B</u> <u>C</u>

After you work out the names of these new notes, play them on the piano.

We now have two new Guide Posts: *High C* and *Low C*.
Here are our five Guide Posts.

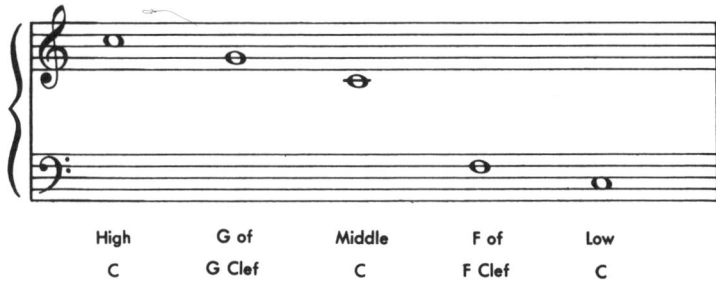

| High C | G of G Clef | Middle C | F of F Clef | Low C |

Let's learn two new words. So far, we have always called this sign 𝄞 a *G Clef*. It has another name—*Treble Clef*. The *F Clef* 𝄢 also has another name—*Bass Clef*.

Remember: *G Clef = Treble Clef*   *F Clef = Bass Clef*

WORK SHEET 7

1. Write in the names of these notes.

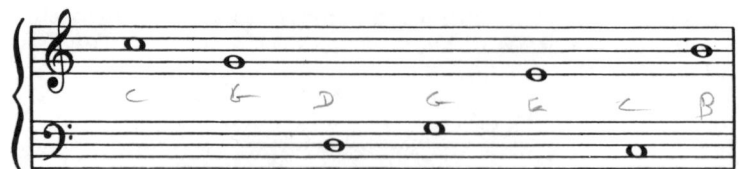

2. Here are some spelling words. See if you can work out what the notes spell.

3. Here are some words for you to write in on the stave. Use semibreves. Write each word twice — once on the Treble Stave and once on the Bass Stave.

FEED   AGED   BEAD   CAFE

4. The bar lines have been left out of the following bars. Be careful to put them in the right places.

LESSON 8
SHARPS

Have you been wondering how to write for the black keys? To do this, we must use a special sign. One of these special signs is called a *Sharp*. It tells us to play the very next key to the right of the one written.

♯

SHARP SIGN

Can you tell the names of these notes? Play them on the piano.

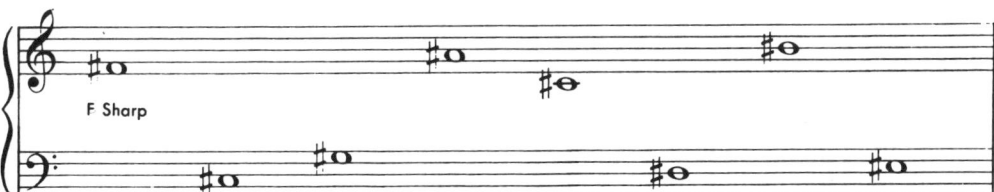

F Sharp

The *Sharp* takes its name from the line or space where the middle section or box is written. Name these sharps.

Are these sharps written in the right place for the notes which follow them?

WORK SHEET 8

1. Place a semibreve after each of the following *Sharps*. Write its name.

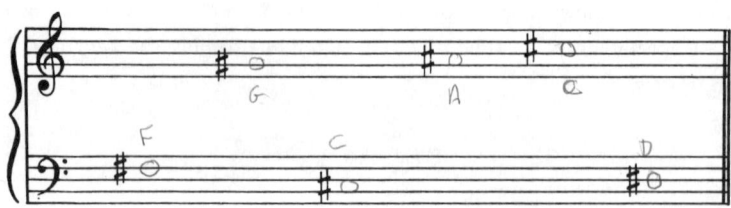

2. Put a *Sharp* in front of each of these notes. Write the names.

3. The time signatures are missing in the following examples. Put them in.

4. Draw a line to connect the things which match.

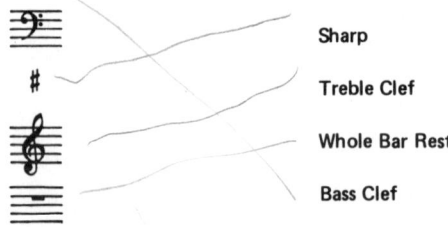

Sharp

Treble Clef

Whole Bar Rest

Bass Clef

LESSON 9
FLATS

We have already had one sign for writing the black keys. Here is the other:

♭

FLAT SIGN

It is called a *Flat* and tells us to play the very next key to the left of the one written.

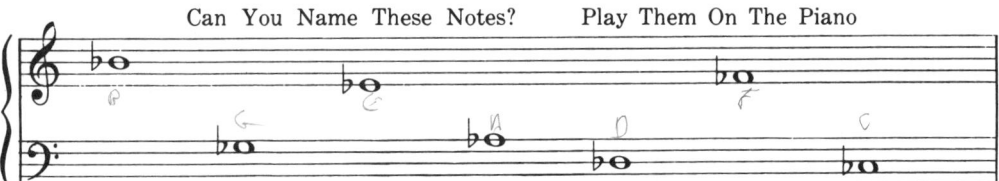

Like the sharps, the *Flats* get their names from the line or space where the closed part is written. Name these *Flats*.

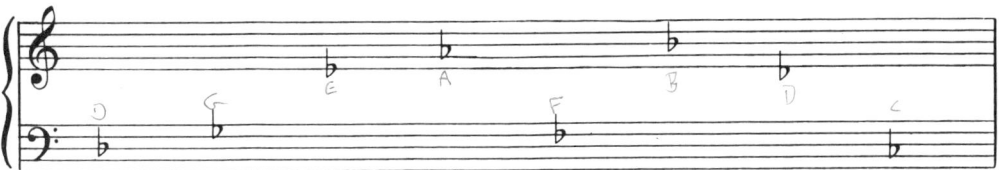

If a sharp or a flat is written next to a note it tells us that that note should be played sharp or flat and that any other note of the same pitch following it in the bar should also be played that way. If, however, the sharp or flat sign is placed between the clef sign and the time signature, it tells us that that note is to be played sharp or flat each time it appears in the piece. This is called the KEY SIGNATURE:

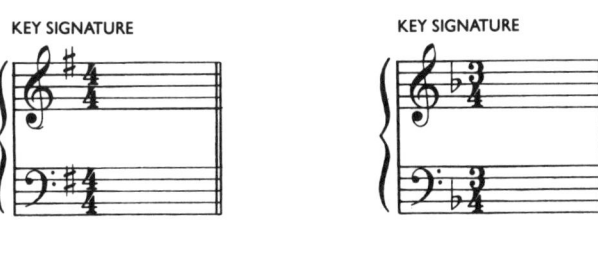

WORK SHEET 9

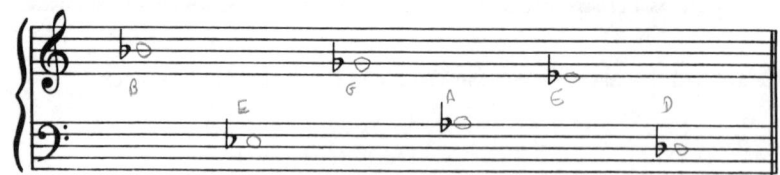

2. Put a circle round every note which is to be played flat.

3. Place each of the following signs on the staff.

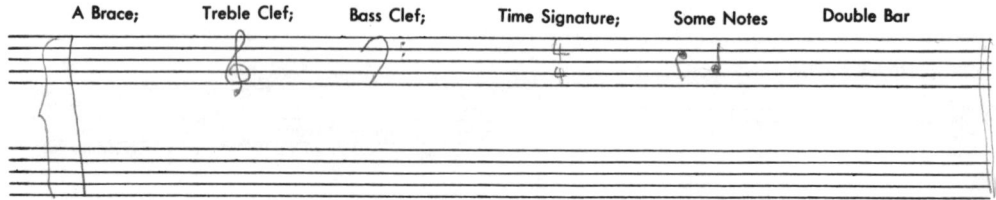

4. How many white keys do we skip in going from one note to the next in the following example? (*Hint*: Count the lines and spaces which are skipped.)

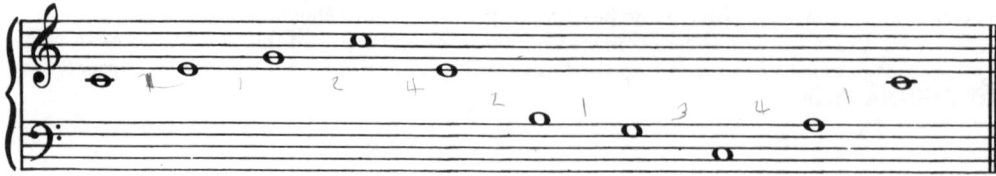

5. Circle the key signatures.

LESSON 10
QUAVERS

You have learned about notes which get one, two, three, and four beats. Now let us learn about a note which gets only half a beat. It is called a *Quaver*.

One *Quaver*   Two or more *Quavers* are connected by a *Beam*   The *Quaver* Rest

Everyone should learn two different ways of counting quavers. Since the beat is divided into two parts, the easiest way is to count it in two parts. Most people say:

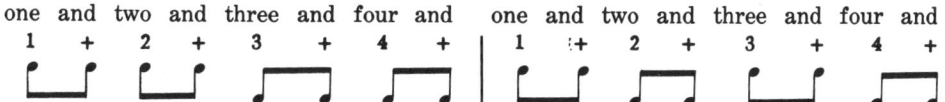

This is very easy to understand when all the notes are eight quavers as in the first example. But even when the quavers are mixed with crotchets and minims it is best to go on counting the "ands" so that all the beats will be alike.

The beats are written in for the first example. Write them in for the other examples and then clap.

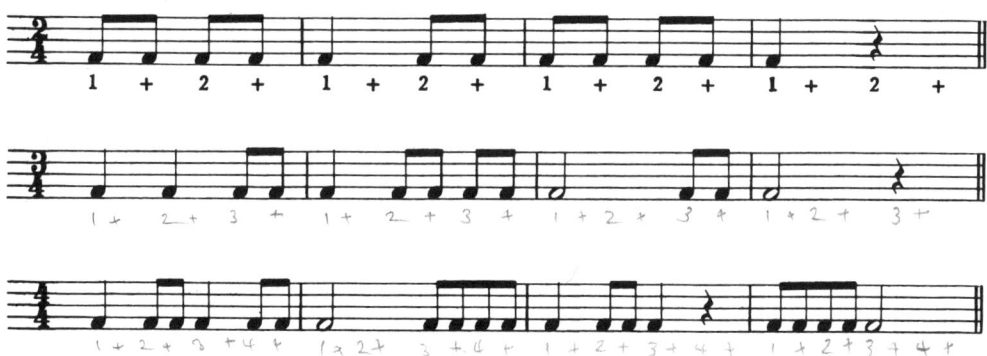

When you can do this without making a mistake you should try to learn the other way of counting quavers. In this second way, we do not count the "ands" — just the numbers. We have to fit the quaver exactly half way between the two numbers.

When you can do this one correctly, go back and try to do the other examples without counting "ands".

WORK SHEET 10

1. Draw: A Quaver Note   A Quaver Rest   Two Quavers connected by a Beam

2. Write in the beats for the following bars using "ands".

3. Write in the beats for these bars without using "ands".

4. Complete these bars by adding one note or one rest.

5. Draw a line to connect the things which match.

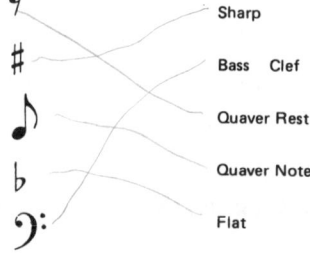

LESSON 11
CURVED LINES AND DOTS

In music, a curved line connects things while a dot shows that they should be separated. If the curved line connects two notes of the same pitch it is called a *Tie* and the notes are spoken of as *Tied Notes*. This means that we play the first one but only count for the second without striking it again. One curved line can tie only two notes. A separate tie must be used to tie each note to the note following it.

When a curved line is placed over or under notes of different pitches it is called a *Slur*. This tells us to hold each note under the slur until we play the next note. There must not be any little rest in between. Musicians call this type of playing *Legato;* an Italian word meaning "bound together". One *Slur* may connect many notes.

When a dot is placed over or under a note it tells us to separate that note from the one which comes next. This is just the opposite of *Legato* playing. The Italian word for this type of playing is *Staccato* which means "separated".

Two important words to remember: *Legato*—Connected   *Staccato*—Separated.

WORK SHEET 11

1. Mark T for tied notes, S for slurs.

2. Draw Ties or Slurs for these notes. Mark them S or T.

3. Put a circle ◯ round the notes which are to be played *Staccato*.

4. Mark the true statements with a T; put an F after the false ones.

    ♩ This note should be played *Staccato*   F
    𝄾 This rest gets one beat in 4/4 time   F
    𝄻 A semibreve rest always gets four beats   F
    ♫ Two Quavers equal one Crotchet   T

5. Write these words in two places on the Grand Stave. Use Crotchets on the upper stave and Minims on the lower stave.

LESSON 12
SOME MORE SIGNS AND ITALIAN WORDS

♮ This sign is called a *Natural*. It cancels a sharp or flat and tells us to play the note as written, disregarding any sharps or flats in the key signature as well as those added in the course of the piece. As with sharps and flats, it affects the note each time it comes in the bar where it is written.

The piano was invented in 1709, or just over 275 years ago. Before that time there were other instruments which looked something like the piano. They had keyboards with white and black keys arranged just as they are on the piano. But there was one big difference. It was impossible to play some notes loud while playing others softly. The piano was the first keyboard instrument able to do this. Its inventor, Cristofori, called it a "Soft-Loud". In Italian the words for soft and loud are *Piano* and *Forte*. Since we call people we know very well by their first names, we now call our instrument by its first name — *Piano* — which means soft. But it is valuable to remember that its full name is *Pianoforte*. This will help us remember the word *Forte*, which means loud.

If a composer wants a note or a section of a piece to be soft he uses the sign *p*, which stands for *Piano*. If he wants us to play loud, he uses the sign *f*, which stands for *Forte*. Remember these words and their signs; look for them in your pieces.

PIANO - *p* - SOFT   FORTE - *f* - LOUD

WORK SHEET 12

1. Place a Natural Sign before each of the following notes on the Grand Stave.

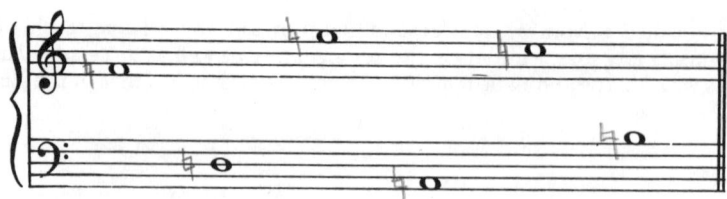

2. Place these signs on the Grand Stave.

A Brace; Treble Clef; Bass Clef; Time Signature; Some Notes; Double Bar

3. Write in the beats for these bars using "ands".

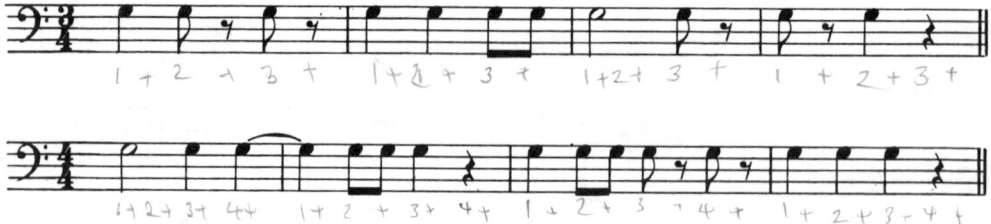

4. Draw the sign for each of the following:

   Legato..........
   Staccato..........
   Loud..........
   Soft..........

LESSON 13
MORE NEW NOTES

We have only a few more notes to learn in order to know all the notes written on the grand stave. And if you remember your musical alphabet they are very easy to work out.

Write in the names of the new notes. Play them on the piano.

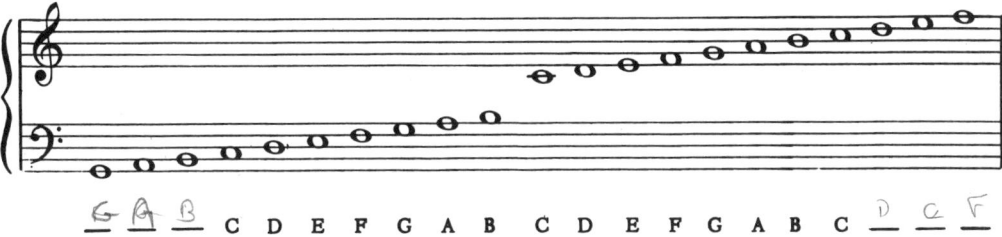

G A B C D E F G A B C D E F G A B C D E F

We now have two more *Guide Posts* for note reading.

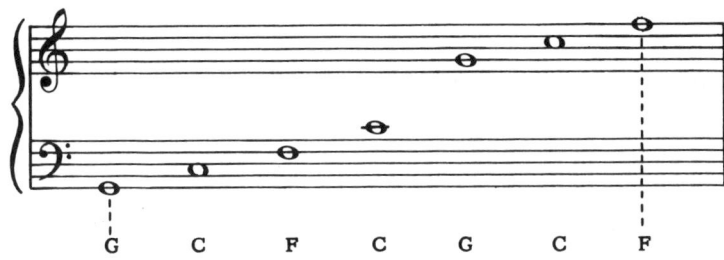

G   C   F   C   G   C   F

When the *Octave Sign* 8·········· is placed over one or more notes, it tells us to play these notes one octave (eight notes) higher than where they were written. If it is placed underneath the notes, it means to play them one octave lower.

WORK SHEET 13

1. Rewrite these notes without the Octave Sign. Be sure that the notes are still the same ones on the keyboard.

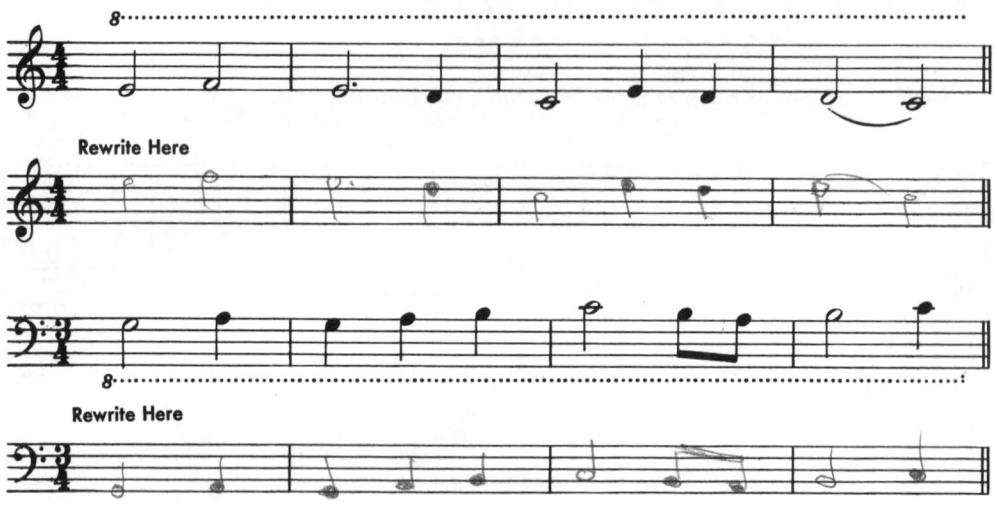

2. Can you work out these spelling words?

3. The Time Signatures have been left out. Can you put in the right ones?

LESSON 14
UPBEATS

So far, all the rhythms we have counted and clapped have started on the first beat of the bar — that is, they have started on the strong beat. We have had these patterns:

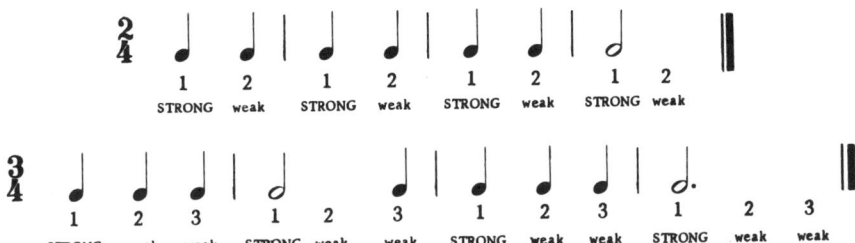

Now we are going to have some patterns which do not start on the strong beat and so do not start from the count of *One*. Since the first beat of the bar is always the strong one and comes after the bar line, we only have to count backwards from the bar line to find what beat to start on.

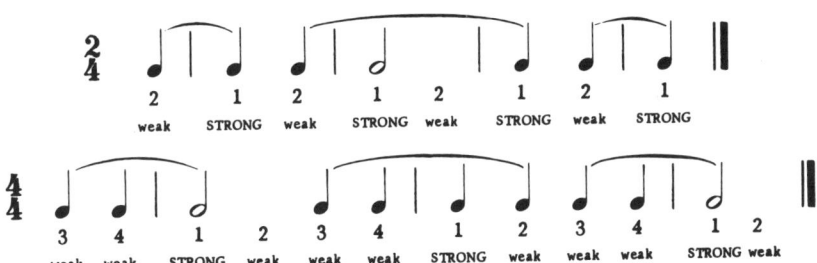

Here are some for you to work out. What beat does each of these examples start on?

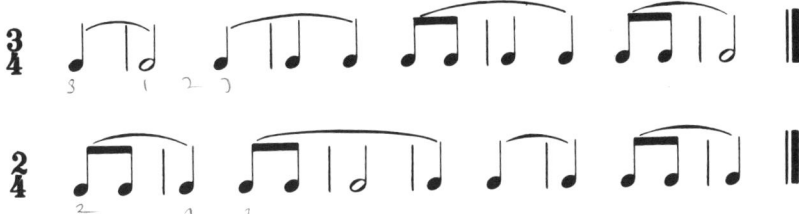

The notes which come before the first bar line are called the *Upbeat* because the conductor of an orchestra always raises his baton before the first beat of the bar.

31

WORK SHEET 14

1. Write in the counting for the following bars.

2. How is your Italian today? Write the English meaning of each of these words.
   Piano   quiet
   Legato   smooth
   Staccato separate
   Forte   loud

3. Rewrite these bars correcting all the mistakes.

LESSON 15
REVIEW WORK SHEET

1. Here are some words written with notes. Work out what they spell.

2. Put in the correct time signatures for these examples.

3. Write three different notes with each of the following letter names.

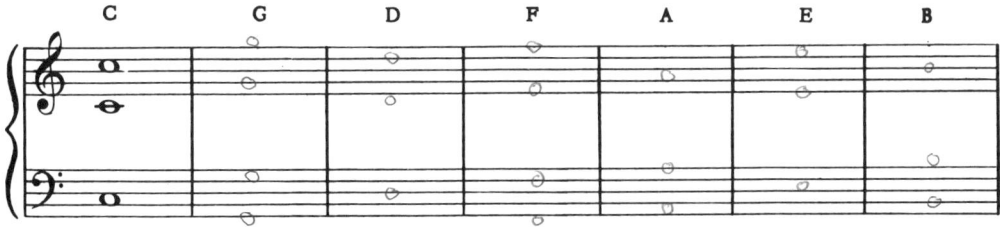

4. Put in the bar lines. Beware of *Upbeats!*

LESSON 15
REVIEW WORK SHEET (Continued)

5. Here is your last chance to match them!

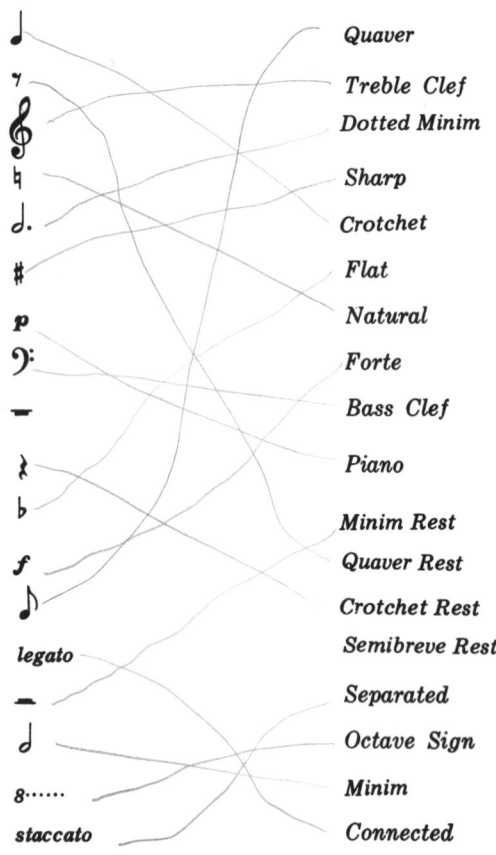

PART TWO
LESSON 1
TONES AND SEMITONES

A semitone is the distance from any key on the piano to its nearest neighbour on the right or left, whether white or black.

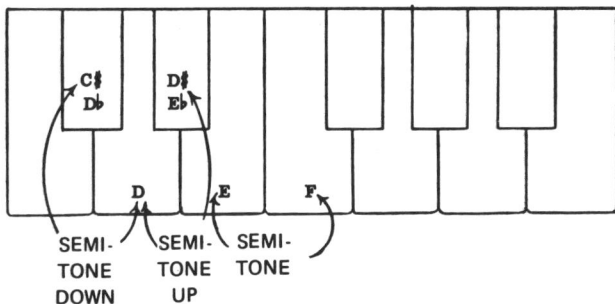

In this case, it does not matter whether we say the semitone is from D to D sharp or from D to E flat. The important thing is that there must not be any keys between the two keys making up the semitone.

Most semitones involve one white key and one black key. However, there are two semitones between white keys. Can you find them? Is it possible to have a semitone between two black keys? Why?

NEW WAY OF EXPLAINING SHARPS AND FLATS: a sharp raises a note one semitone; a flat lowers a tone one semitone.

How many semitones are there in an octave? If we play all the semitones in an octave, we are playing a *Chromatic Scale*.

Two semitones equal one whole tone. We must always skip one key in playing a whole tone.

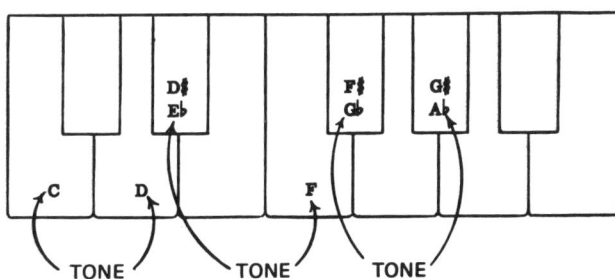

Is there always a tone between two neighbouring white keys? Is there always a tone between two black keys? Can you play a tone from a white key to a black one?

How many tones are there in an octave? If we start from any key and play tones until we reach the octave of that note, we are playing a *Whole Tone Scale*.

WORK SHEET 1

1. Mark an X on the keys one semitone above and one semitone below the keys marked here.

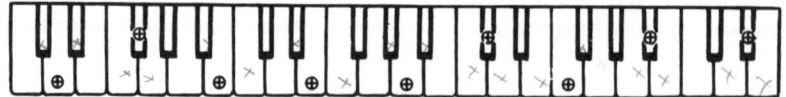

Mark an X on the keys a tone above and a tone below the ones marked here.

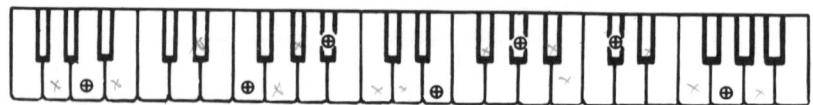

2. Mark the semitones S, the tones T.

3. Do the next exercise without looking at the keyboard!

   a) Write the names of the notes one semitone below and one semitone above each of these notes.
   F#..G.G#., Eb.E.F., B.C.C#, Ab.A.A#, C.D flat.D., E.F.F#., A.A sharp.B.

   b) Write the names of the notes a tone below and a tone above each of these notes.
   G.A.B., C.D.E., D.E.F#., F.G sharp.A#., Ab.B flat.C., Cb.F.G., B.D flat.Eb.

   c) The white key semitones fall between ..B.. and ..C.., and between ..E.. and ..F..
   d) The black key tones come between C#.. and D#.., between F#.. and G#.., and between G#.. and A#..

4. Write a note a tone above each note written here.

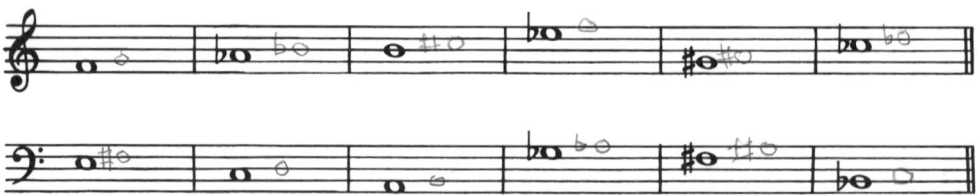

36

LESSON 2
LEDGER LINES

You have already learned the names of all the lines and spaces of the grand stave, but even by using the octave signs we are not yet at the ends of the keyboard. To write these notes, we must add more lines above and below the grand stave. These lines are called *Ledger Lines* and are just large enough to write one note. Remember that the ledger lines and the spaces in between are in alphabetical order just as the lines and spaces of the grand staff.

Write the names of the new notes. Notice that *High C* is on the second ledger line above the treble stave, while *Low C* is on the second ledger line below the bass stave. These are two important new guide posts.

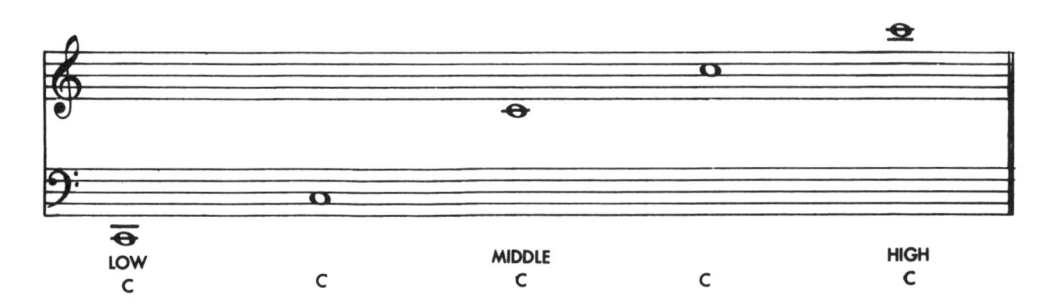

How many ledger lines would it take to write the top note on the piano? The bottom note? Middle C is a ledger line between the two staffs. We sometimes write other notes on ledger lines between the two staffs of the grand stave.

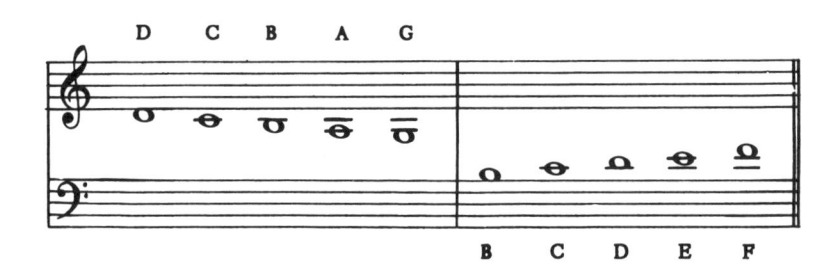

WORK SHEET 2

1. Write the names of these notes.

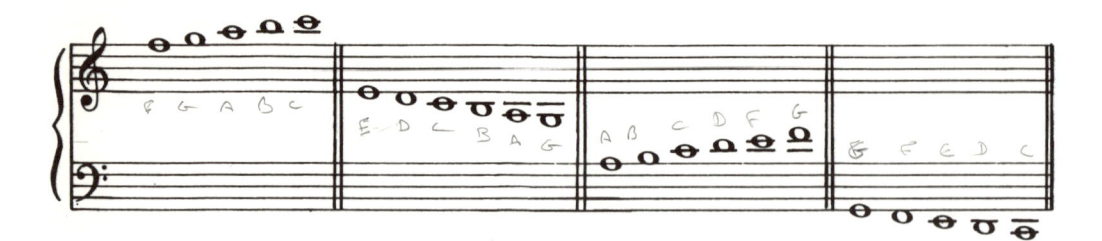

2. Here are some spelling words using leger lines.

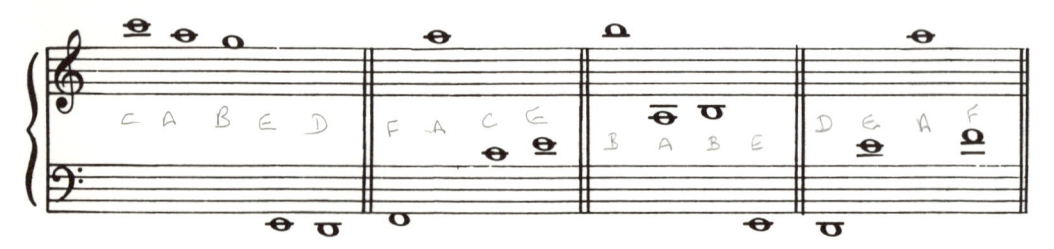

3. Write five different Cs and four of each of the other notes.

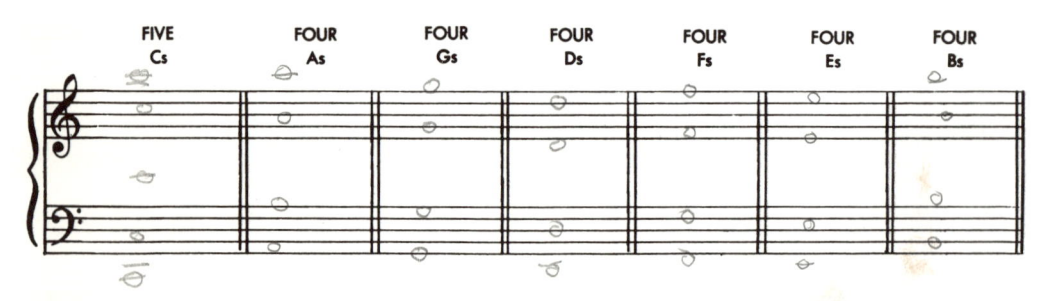

4. Write the note a semitone above each of these notes.

LESSON 3
SCALES

Our word *Scale* comes from the Italian word *Scala*, which means a staircase or step ladder. In music, a *Scale* is a succession of notes starting from any note and moving *By Step* to the note an octave higher (or lower). You have already learned that a chromatic scale moves by semitones and that a whole-tone scale moves by tones. Most scales are made up of some semitones and some tones.

The white keys from middle C up to the next C make up the *C Major Scale*. It is the only major scale using only white keys. How many half steps are there in the C Major Scale? How many tones?

The pattern of tones and semitones between the two Cs is called *The Major Scale Pattern*.

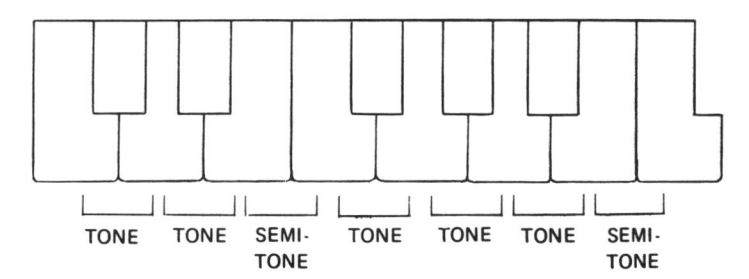

TONE   TONE   SEMI-TONE   TONE   TONE   TONE   SEMI-TONE

If we start on any key on the piano and follow that pattern of tones and semitones we will be playing a major scale. Play a major scale starting on F; on G; on D. (Play the first four notes with the left hand and the last four with the right hand.) Just be careful to follow the *Major Scale Pattern*.

TONE   TONE   SEMI-TONE   TONE   TONE   TONE   SEMI-TONE

The scale gets its name from the note on which we start the pattern. This note is called the *Key Note*, the *Home Note*, or *Tonic*. The scale does not sound complete unless it ends on the *Key Note*. The major scale which has B Flat for its Tonic is a B Flat Major Scale.

Since all the piano keys are the same width at the back, we can make a pattern of the major scale. Place the pattern so that the number 1 is behind the key on which you wish to start your scale. Then play the notes indicated by the numbers and you will have a major scale. But you must also learn to play the scale by remembering the pattern of tones and semitones.

| 1 | 2 | 3 | 4 | 5 | 6 | 7 | 8 |

WORK SHEET 3

1. a) What is a scale? _a pattern of tones & semi-tones_

   b) Between which notes of the C Major Scale do the semitones fall? _E_ and _F_ ; _B_ and _C_
   c) Write the major scale pattern. _t – t – s – t – t – t – s_
   d) Give three other names for the first note of the scale. _key note, home note, tonic_
   e) Where does a major scale get its name? _pattern of t's & s's ?_

2. Write the note a tone above each note written here.

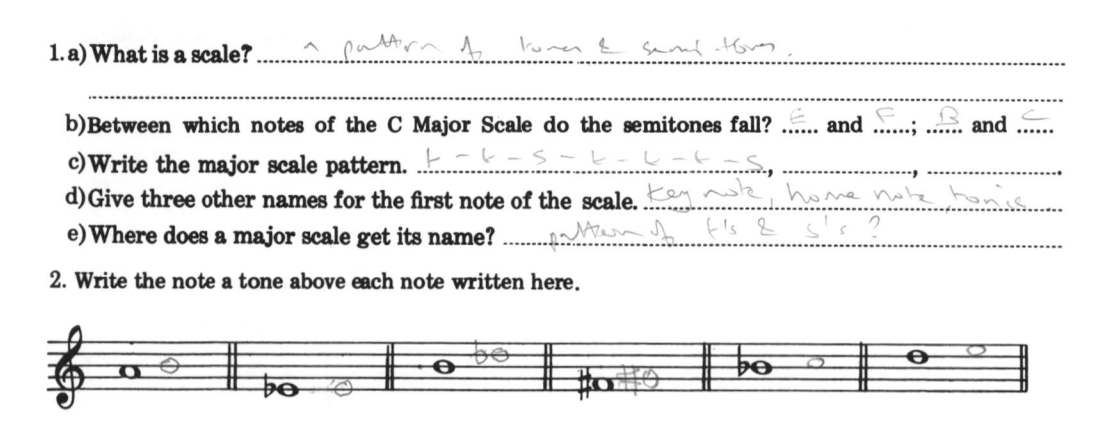

Write the note a semitone above each note written here.

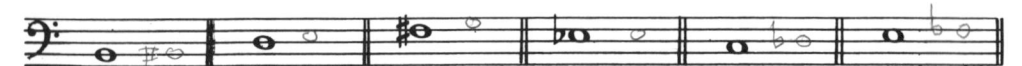

3. Write a chromatic scale starting on G. Use sharps for the black keys.

Write a descending chromatic scale starting on E. Use flats for the black keys.

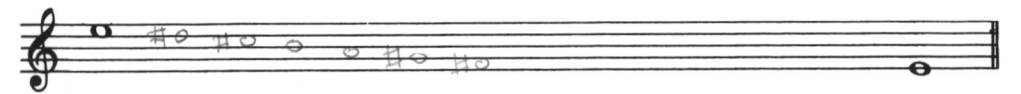

4. Here is a review of counting. Write in the beats for these examples using "ands" for the first one and doing the other one without "ands". Use + for "and".

LESSON 4
SCALE DEGREES AND TETRACHORDS

If we say that the semitones fall between E and F and between B and C, we are speaking of only the C Major Scale. But if we say that the semitones fall between the third and fourth notes and between the seventh and eighth notes, we are speaking of all major scales. Since all major scales have the same pattern of tones and semitones, we frequently use numbers to represent the notes. These numbers are called the *Scale Degrees*. The scale degrees of any major scale are the numbers 1, 2, 3, 4, 5, 6, 7, and 8.

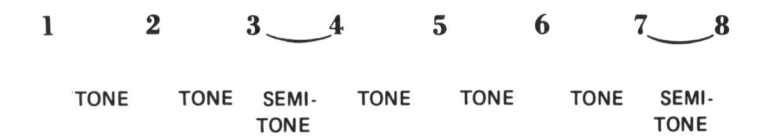

1	2	3	4	5	6	7	8
TONE	TONE	SEMI-TONE	TONE	TONE	TONE	SEMI-TONE	

The semitones always come between 3 and 4 and between 7 and 8 in a major scale. When writing the scale degrees, mark the semitones with a slur. Play an A Major Scale. Divide the notes between the two hands, playing the first four notes with the left hand and the last four with the right hand, as you did in the last lesson. Notice that each hand plays *Tone, Tone, Semitone*. These half scales are called *Tetrachords*.

The major scale is made up of two tetrachords. Each has the pattern of *Tone, Tone, Semitone*. There is a tone between the two tetrachords.

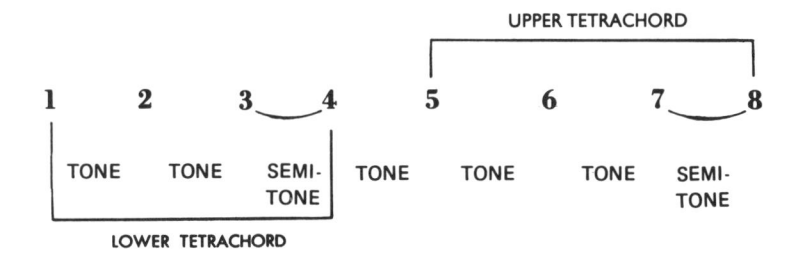

```
                                    UPPER TETRACHORD
                                 ┌──────────────────────┐
   1     2     3 ‿ 4     5     6     7 ‿ 8
   │ TONE  TONE  SEMI- │ TONE  TONE  TONE  SEMI-
   │              TONE │                     TONE
   └───────────────────┘
       LOWER TETRACHORD
```

You must know all of the material presented in this lesson and in Lesson 3 thoroughly before you can move on to Lesson 5 where you will start writing scales on the stave. If you are not sure of the Major Scale Pattern, Scale Degrees, and Tetrachords, review Lessons 3 and 4.

WORK SHEET 4

1. a) What are the degrees of the major scale? ... 1, 2, 3, 4, 5, 6, 7, 8
   b) How many tetrachords are there in a major scale? ... 2
   c) What is the pattern of the lower tetrachord? ... T, T, S
   d) What is the pattern of the upper tetrachord? ... T, T, S
   e) What kind of step is there between the two tetrachords? ... T
   f) Write the degrees of the major scale. Mark the semitones with slurs. Underneath this, write the major scale pattern. Put a circle around each tetrachord.

   1 2 3 4 5 6 7 8
   T T S T T T S

2. Form a major scale tetrachord on each of these notes.

3. Here are some spelling words.

   C A G E   B E G G E D   A D A G E   F A C E

LESSON 5
WRITING THE MAJOR SCALE

The major scale is a *Diatonic Scale*. This means that the eight notes have letter names in alphabetical order. Each letter of the musical alphabet is used only once, except the tonic which is repeated as the final note. Since the lines and spaces of the grand stave are also in alphabetical order, the first thing to do in writing a scale is to write in the eight notes on eight consecutive lines and spaces. Start with the key tone and go to its octave.

Next, write in the numbers from 1 to 8 indicating the scale degrees. Mark the semitones with slurs. If the tonic has a sharp or flat, be sure to repeat it when writing the final note.

As the final step, go back and put in the sharps or flats to make up the major scale pattern. By writing the notes on the stave before putting in the sharps or flats, we make sure that each note will have the correct letter name.

This helps us to understand why a key is sometimes called by its sharp name and sometimes by its flat name. Let us take G sharp and A flat as an example. In the key A Major, the seventh note is the black key between G and A. Since the seventh step of the A Major scale must have G for its letter name, it must be G Sharp. In the scale of E Flat Major, the fourth note is once again the black key between G and A. But the fourth note of the E Flat scale must have A for its letter name, so it must be A flat.

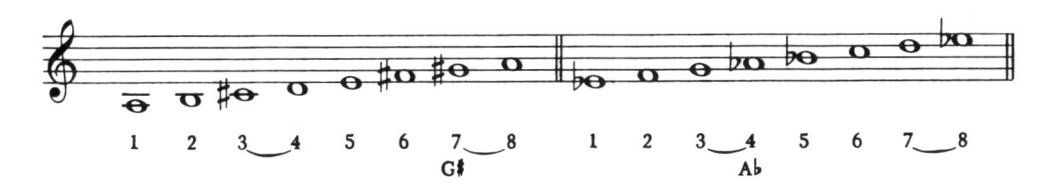

WORK SHEET 5

1. Write the numbers of the scale degrees under the notes of these scales. Mark the semitones with slurs. Then put in the sharps or flats needed to make up the major scale pattern.

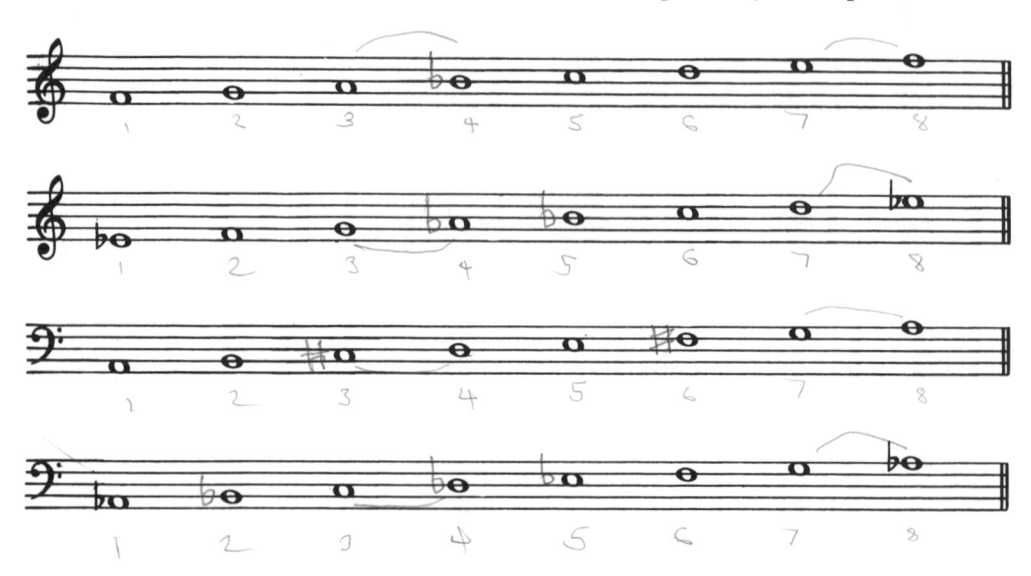

2. Write the following scales. Be sure to write the notes on the stave first. Then put in the scale degrees and finally, put in the necessary sharps or flats.

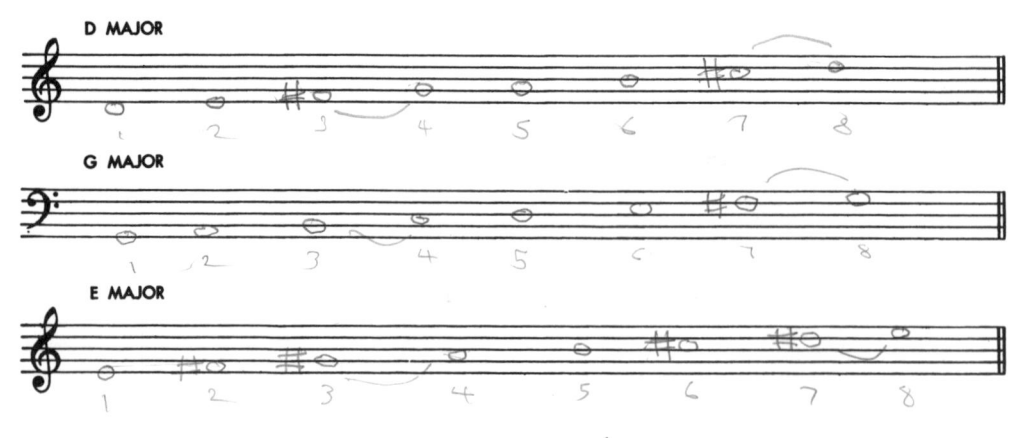

   D MAJOR

   G MAJOR

   E MAJOR

3. a) What is the fourth degree of the G Major Scale? C ; of the E Major Scale? A .
   b) What is the third degree of the D Major Scale? F# ; of the A Major Scale? C# .
   c) What is the seventh degree of the F Major Scale? E ; of the E Flat Major Scale? D .
   d) What is the sixth degree of the B Flat Major Scale? G ; of the C Major Scale? A .

LESSON 6
DOTTED CROTCHET

In PART ONE, LESSON 2 (p.7) you learned that a dot placed after a note always gets half as many beats as the note itself. So far, the only dotted note we have used has been the dotted minim. Now it is time to learn about another dotted note – the *Dotted Crotchet*.

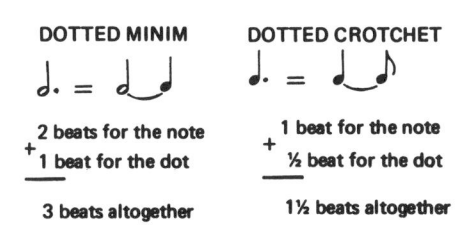

DOTTED MINIM

𝅗𝅥. = 𝅗𝅥 𝅘𝅥

  2 beats for the note
+ 1 beat for the dot
  _____
  3 beats altogether

DOTTED CROTCHET

𝅘𝅥. = 𝅘𝅥 𝅘𝅥𝅮

  1 beat for the note
+ ½ beat for the dot
  _____
  1½ beats altogether

Here are some common patterns using dotted crotchets. The beats have been written in for the first example. Write in the beats for the other examples using "and". Count out loud and clap. When you are sure of the rhythms, try clapping while counting only the numbers.

[Musical example in 3/4 time]
1+ 2 + 3 +   1 + 2 + 3 +   1 + 2 + 3 +   1 + 2 + 3 +   1+2+3+

[Musical example in 4/4 time]
3+ 4+   1+ 2+ 3+ 4+   1 + 2 + 3 + 4 +   1 + 2+ 3+4+   1 + 2+

[Musical example in 2/4 time]
1 + 2+   1+ 2+   1 + 2 +   1+ 2+   1 + 2+   1 + 2+   1+2+

[Musical example in 4/4 time]
1+ 2+ 3 + 4 +   1 + 2+ 3 +4+   1 + 2 + 3 +4+   1 + 2+3 +4+

Notice that in all of these examples the dotted crotchet was followed by a quaver note or a quaver rest. Since the dotted crotchet received one and a half beats, we need the half beat of a quaver note or quaver rest to make up two full beats.

45

WORK SHEET 6

1. Write in the beats for the following bars using "ands"

2. Write in the beats for the following bars without "ands".

3. Write the following scales.

   A MAJOR

   Eb MAJOR

4. Fill these bars with as many quavers as necessary to give the right number of beats.

LESSON 7
INTERVALS

An *Interval* is the distance between two notes. We measure intervals by counting the number of letters involved, including the names of the two notes of the interval. In order to know the interval from C to E, count the letter names C, D, and E. Since there are three letters, the interval is a third. From D to A is a fifth, because there are five letter names — D, E, F, G, and A. In naming intervals, we count from the bottom note to the top one, naming the bottom one first. The interval from F to D means the interval from F up to D, not F down to D.

What is the interval from B to E? From C to B?

fourth   seventh.

WRITING INTERVALS ON THE STAVE
Since each line and each space of the grand stave represents one letter name, we can also measure intervals by counting the lines and spaces from one to the other. This also makes it easy to write intervals on the staff.

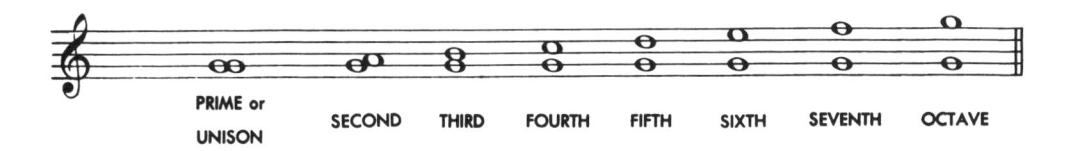

PRIME or UNISON   SECOND   THIRD   FOURTH   FIFTH   SIXTH   SEVENTH   OCTAVE

Notice that when the interval is a unison, a third, a fifth, or a seventh, both notes are on lines or both notes are in spaces. For seconds, fourths, sixths, and octaves, one is always on a line, the other in a space.

If you play every other white key on the piano, you are playing in thirds. Can you say the musical alphabet in thirds?

At this time we are only interested in the number names of intervals, such as a fifth, a second, etc. You will gradually learn to distinguish between different intervals with the same number of letter names. For the number names of intervals, sharps and flats do not matter. From A to G is a seventh; from A to G flat is also a seventh; from A to G sharp is still a seventh.

WORK SHEET 7

1. Write the note which is the required interval above each of the following notes.

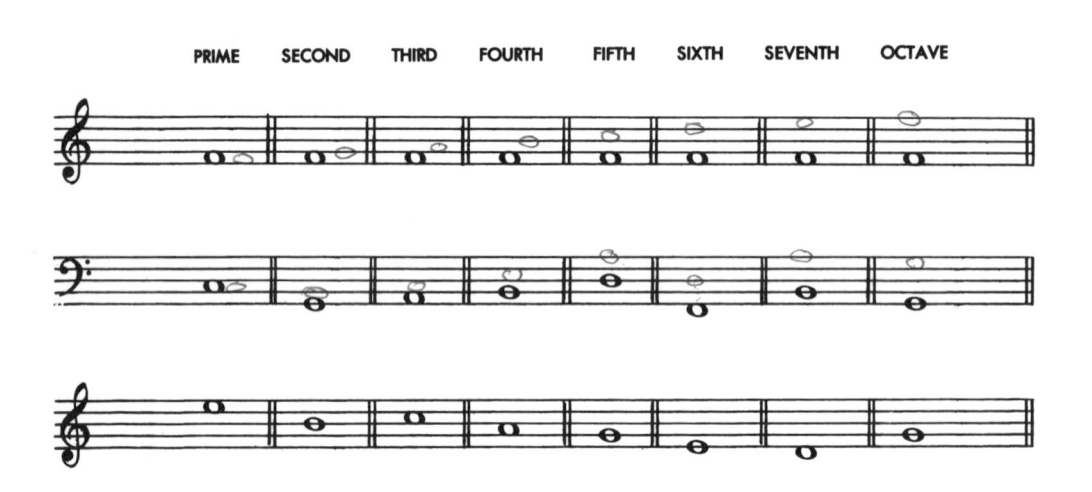

PRIME   SECOND   THIRD   FOURTH   FIFTH   SIXTH   SEVENTH   OCTAVE

2. Identify each of the following intervals.

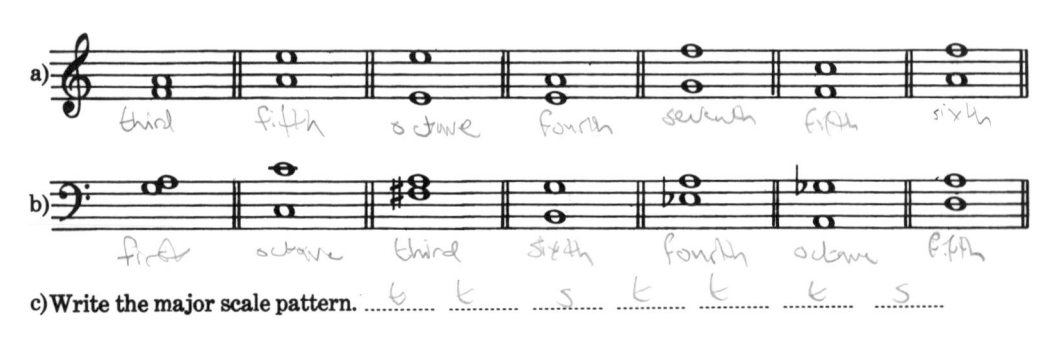

a) third, fifth, octave, fourth, seventh, fifth, sixth

b) first, octave, third, sixth, fourth, octave, fifth

c) Write the major scale pattern. t   t   s   t   t   t   s

3. Here are some spelling words.

BEADED   EGAD   FACADE   EDGE

LESSON 8
SIX EIGHT TIME

So far, all of the exercises you have had, have had time signatures with 4 for the bottom number. There have been many examples in $\frac{2}{4}$, $\frac{3}{4}$ and $\frac{4}{4}$ time. In all of these, a crotchet received one beat. That is what the 4 on the bottom of the time signature tells us.

Now we are going to have time signatures with 8 on the bottom. $\frac{6}{8}$ and $\frac{3}{8}$ are the most common. In any kind of time with 8 for the bottom number, *a quaver gets one beat*.

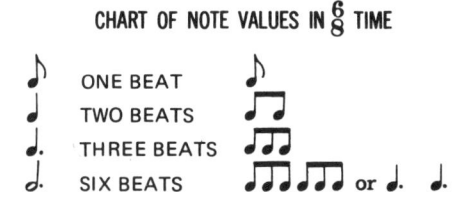

CHART OF NOTE VALUES IN $\frac{6}{8}$ TIME

♪ ONE BEAT
♩ TWO BEATS
♩. THREE BEATS
♩.. SIX BEATS

It is important to understand the difference between the six quavers in $\frac{6}{8}$ time and the six quavers in $\frac{3}{4}$ time. In $\frac{6}{8}$ time, the six quavers are linked together in groups of three. In $\frac{3}{4}$ time, the quavers come in three groups of two so that we can still see the three crotchets in the bar.

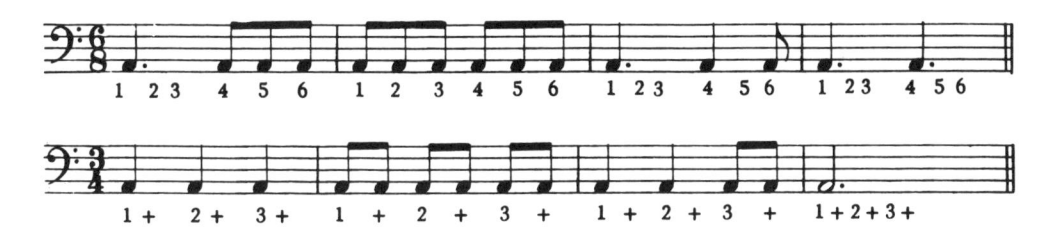

Since the six quavers in $\frac{6}{8}$ time are grouped in threes, the dotted crotchet is very important in this kind of time.

Write in the beats and clap these bars in $\frac{6}{8}$ time and $\frac{3}{8}$ time.

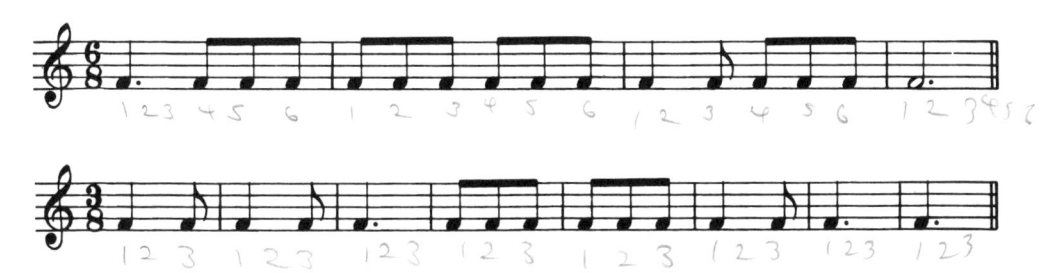

WORK SHEET 8

1. Write in the beats for these bars.

(handwritten beats under bars)
Line 1: 1 2 3 4 5 6 | 1 2 3 4 5 6 | 1 2 3 4 5 6 | 1 2 3 4 5 6
Line 2: 1 2 3 | 1 2 3 | 1 2 3 | 1 2 3 | 1 2 3 | 1 2 3 | 1 2 3 | 1 2 3
Line 3: 4 5 6 | 1 2 3 4 5 6 | 1 2 3 4 5 6 | 1 2 3 4 5 6 | 1 2 3

2. Draw a line to connect each note to the number of beats it receives in 6/8 time.

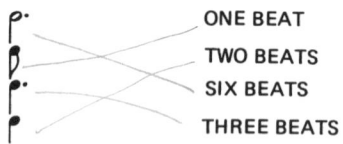

- ♩. — ONE BEAT
- ♩ — TWO BEATS
- ♪. — SIX BEATS
- ♪ — THREE BEATS

3. The time signatures have been left out of these examples. Some are in 6/8 time; the others are in 3/4 time. Be careful to put in the correct signature for each one!

a) 6/8
b) 3/4
c) 3/4
d) 6/8

4. Identify these intervals.

third, octave, fifth, first, fourth, seventh, sixth

LESSON 9
KEY SIGNATURES

Now that you have learned to write major scales, you must learn the key signatures which come from the scales. In studying keys and key signatures, three things are most important:

1) The order in which the sharps and flats are written.
2) The correct number of sharps or flats for the different keys.
3) How to tell the key by seeing the key signature.

Here are the scales using one, two, three, and four sharps written with key signatures.

F♯ is always first. Then follow C♯, G♯, and D♯ in that order. The key note is on the line or in the space above the last sharp.

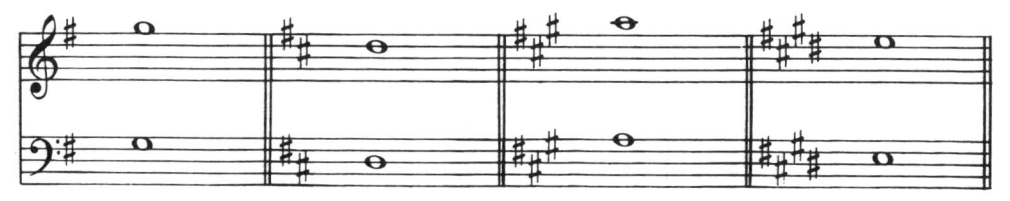

Here are the scales using one, two, three, and four flats.

B♭ is always first. Then follow E♭, A♭, and D♭ in that order. Remember the word "BEAD" for the first four flats. The key note is always the next-to-last flat. The key with only one flat is F major.

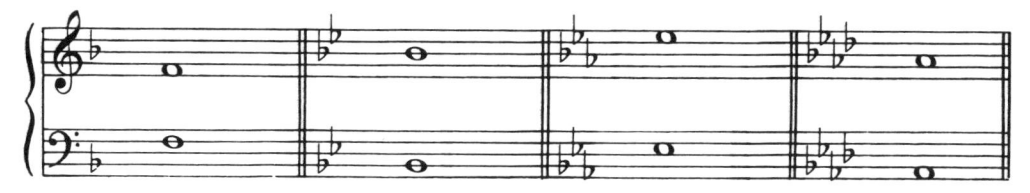

WORK SHEET 9

1. Write the sharps in correct order. ...... F ...... C ...... G ...... D ......
   Write the flats in the correct order. ...... B ...... E ...... A ...... D ......
2. Write the following key signatures. Indicate the key note.

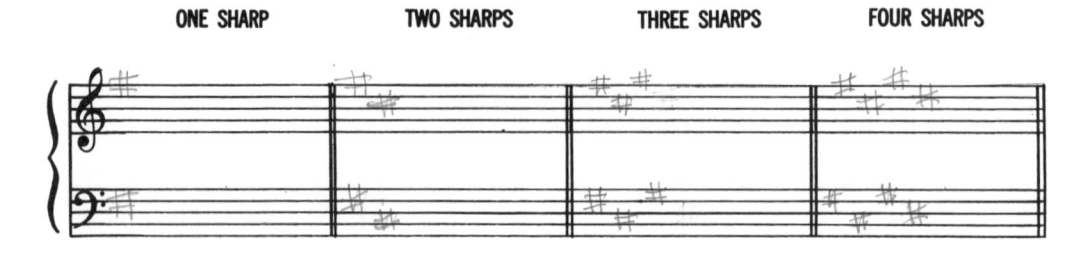

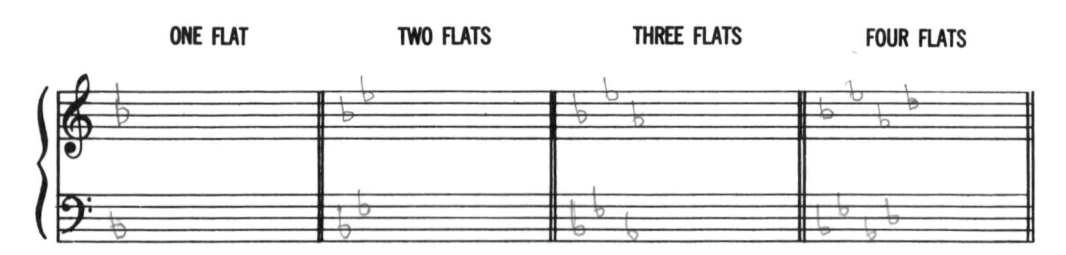

   ONE SHARP   TWO SHARPS   THREE SHARPS   FOUR SHARPS

   ONE FLAT   TWO FLATS   THREE FLATS   FOUR FLATS

3. Write the key signature of each of the following keys.
   a) G Major ...... #
   b) B Flat Major ...... b b
   c) A Major ...... # # #
   d) F Major ...... b
   e) E Major ...... # # # #
   f) D Major ...... # #
   g) A Flat Major ...... b b b b
   h) E Flat Major ...... b b b

   bb c d be
   a b c# d e f# g a
   e f# g# a b c# d
   d e f# g a b c# d
   ab Bb c db eb f g ab
   eb f g ab bb c d eb

4. Write the name of the note which has the sharp, flat or natural next to it in each of these chords.

   C#   Eb   D   B   G#   Eb   Ab   C

LESSON 10
MAJOR TRIADS

When we strike several notes at one time, we are playing a chord. A chord made up of three notes arranged in thirds is called a *Triad*. This word is easy to remember if you keep in mind that a tricycle has three wheels and a triangle has three corners. *Tri*, the first part of all of these words, comes from a Greek word meaning three.

Say the musical alphabet in thirds. This is the chord alphabet, because most chords are built in thirds. Remember that the lines of the staff are arranged in thirds, as are the spaces.

A Major Triad is made up of the first, third and fifth notes of a major scale. These notes are then called the *Root*, the *Third*, and the *Fifth* of the major triad.

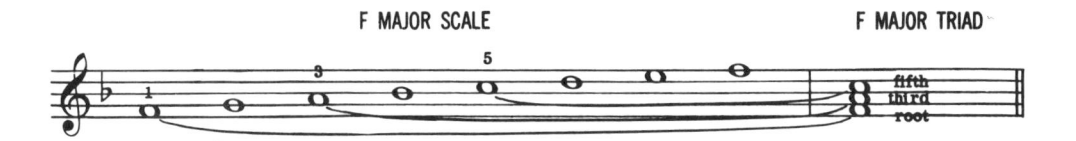

The triad takes its name from the root.

It is possible to build a triad on any note, just as it was possible to start a scale on any note. Build a major triad on each step of the chromatic scale. How many have only white keys? How many have only black keys?

If all the notes of a chord are played at one time, it is called a *Solid* or *Block* chord. If the notes are played one after another, it is called a *Broken Chord* or *Arpeggio*.

WORK SHEET 10

1. a) Write the musical alphabet in thirds starting with D. D. F A C E G B
   b) What is a chord? Several notes played at once
   c) What is a triad? a chord of three notes.
   d) Which notes of the major scale make up the major triad? first, third, and fifth.

2. Build a major triad on each of these notes. Be careful to have all three notes on lines or all three in spaces! Add sharps or flats as needed.

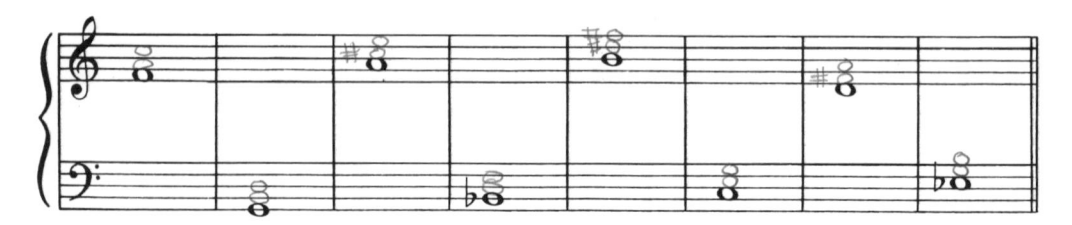

3. Write three major triads which use only white keys; one which uses only black keys.

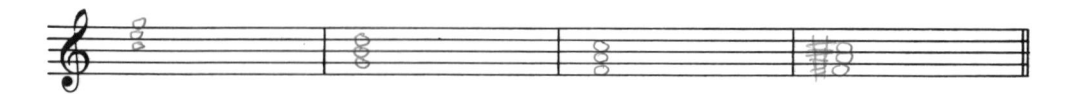

4. Write the key signature of the following keys.

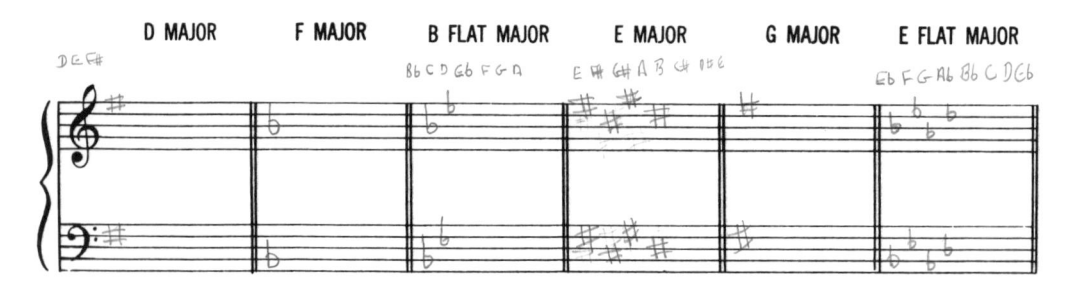

   D MAJOR   F MAJOR   B FLAT MAJOR   E MAJOR   G MAJOR   E FLAT MAJOR

   D E F#
                          Bb C D Eb F G A   E F# G# A B C# D#E   Eb F G Ab Bb C D Eb

5. Rewrite each of these solid chords as a broken chord.

LESSON 11
SOME MORE INTERVALS

So far you have used only number names for identifying intervals. However, there are some intervals you have used so often that you should now learn their exact names. To distinguish between intervals with the same number names, we must know the number of semitones.

When you studied tones and semitones, you were learning about two different kinds of seconds. A tone is a larger second than a semitone. The words *Major* and *Minor* mean *Larger* and *Smaller*. A tone is a *Major Second*; a semitone is a *Minor Second*. (In order to be a minor second, the semitone must use two different letter names — from E to F, or from C to D Flat. If only one letter name is used, as from C to C♯ or from E Flat to E, the interval is called a chromatic semitone and is not a second at all).

Major Second   Minor Second   Minor Second   Chromatic Semitone

Remember that a minor second is a semitone; a major second is a tone.

We used two very important intervals in playing and writing major triads. From the root to the third of a major triad is always a *Major Third*. It has four semitones (or two tones).

MAJOR THIRDS

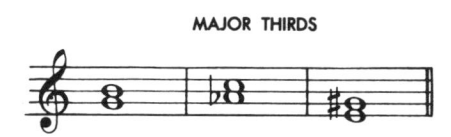

From the root to the fifth of a major triad is always a *Perfect Fifth*. There are seven semitones (or three tones and a semitone) in a perfect fifth. This is also the distance from the first note of the major scale to the fifth note.

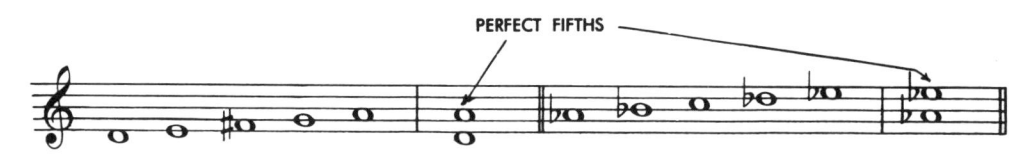

PERFECT FIFTHS

REMEMBER THESE INTERVALS:	MINOR SECOND	MAJOR SECOND	MAJOR THIRD	PERFECT FIFTH
	one semitone	two semitones	four semitones	seven semitones

55

WORK SHEET 11

1. How many semitones make up each of these intervals?
   a) A minor second ...1... A perfect fifth ...7... A major third ...4... A major second ...2...
   b) What do the words major and minor mean? ...larger... and ...smaller...
2. Write the note a perfect fifth above each of these notes.

   Write the note a major third above each of these notes.

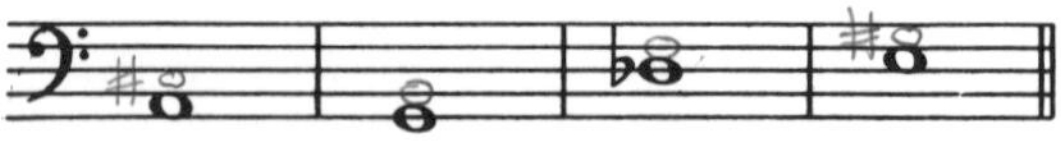

3. Complete the following table by writing the note which is the required interval from the given note.

   MAJOR SECONDS

   MINOR SECONDS

   CHROMATIC SEMITONES

4. Give the exact name of each of these intervals.

   major third — minor second — perfect fifth — major second — perfect fifth

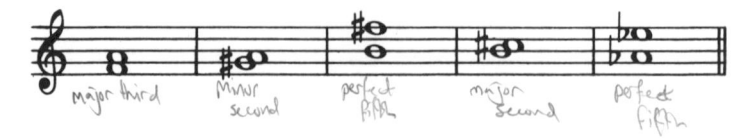

5. Write in the beats for these examples. Use "ands" if you need them.

   4 1 2 3 4 | 1 2 3 4 | 1 2 3 4 | 1 2 3

   1 2 3 4 5 6 | 1 2 3 4 5 6 | 1 2 3 4 5 6 | 1 2 3 4 5 6

LESSON 12
SEMIQUAVERS

A *Semiquaver* is a black note with two flags. Since it takes two semi-quavers to equal one quaver and four semiquavers to equal one crotchet, they usually come in groups — of two, four, six.

Notice that the difference in appearance between semiquavers and quavers is the double flag or beam for the semiquaver.

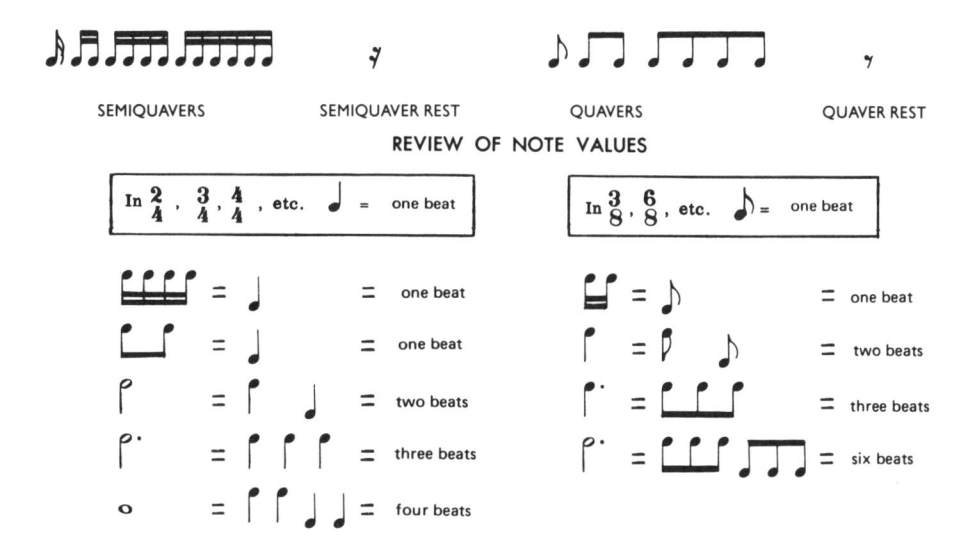

SEMIQUAVERS   SEMIQUAVER REST   QUAVERS   QUAVER REST

REVIEW OF NOTE VALUES

Here are some examples of common rhythms using semiquavers. Write in the beats and clap. Always use "ands" in counting semiquavers. Sometimes it is even necessary to divide the beat still more — 1 a + a 2 a + a, etc. Use "ands" in these bars.

WORK SHEET 12

1. Write in the beats for these bars.

2. Mark the following intervals as Maj. 2nd, Min. 2nd, Maj. 3rd, Perf. 5th. Cross out any other intervals.

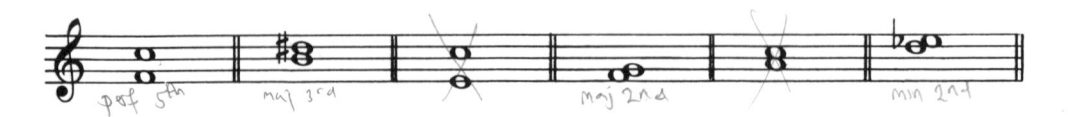

3. Write the following key signatures. Indicate the Tonic.

    G MAJOR   A MAJOR   B♭ MAJOR   A♭ MAJOR

4. Write the following major triads.

    F MAJOR   D MAJOR   E♭ MAJOR   E MAJOR   C MAJOR

LESSON 13
TONIC AND DOMINANT

If you build a white-key triad on each step of the C Major scale, you will find that only three are major triads. Only the ones on the first, fourth, and fifth degrees are major, and we are only interested in the ones on the first and fifth degrees at this time.

I   IV   V

The first degree of the scale is called the *Tonic*. The triad built on the first degree of the scale is called the *Tonic Triad*. Most pieces start with a tonic triad and almost all pieces end with either the tonic note or a tonic triad. You can see how important it is in any key.

The fifth degree of the scale is called the *Dominant*. The word *Dominant* means "of greatest importance". You will soon learn how important the dominant is in the music you play. The triad on the fifth degree of the scale is called the *Dominant Triad*.

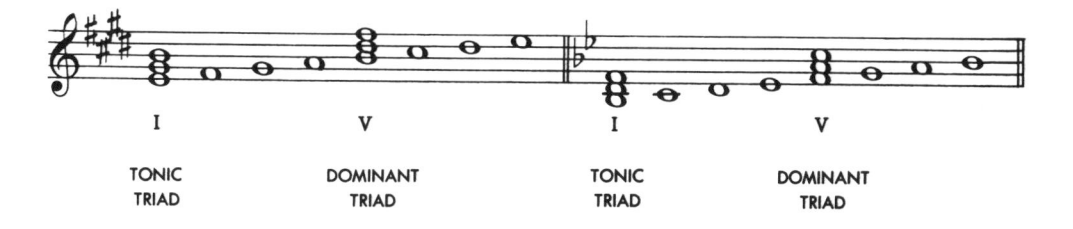

I	V	I	V
TONIC TRIAD	DOMINANT TRIAD	TONIC TRIAD	DOMINANT TRIAD

We represent the notes of the scale by the numbers 1, 2, 3, 4, 5, 6, 7, and 8, the scale degrees. When we speak of the chords which are built on the different degrees of the scale, we use Roman numerals. The chord on the first degree of the scale, the tonic triad, is represented by the Roman numeral I. The chord on the fifth degree of the scale, the dominant, is represented by the Roman numeral V.

IMPORTANT: The first degree of the scale — the *Tonic*.
　　　　　　　The fifth degree of the scale — the *Dominant*.

　　　　　　　The triad built on the *Tonic*—The *Tonic Triad*—represented by I.
　　　　　　　The triad built on the *Dominant*—The *Dominant Triad*—represented by V.

WORK SHEET 13

1. a) The triad built on the first step of the scale is called the ~~tonic~~ triad.
   b) The triad built on the fifth step of the scale is called the ~~dominant~~ triad.
2. Write the following major scales. Mark the first degree of the scale I and the fifth degree V. Then build a major triad on each.

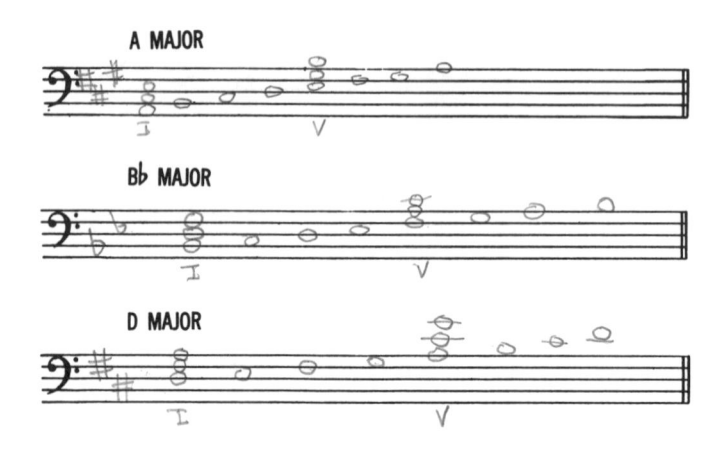

A MAJOR

Bb MAJOR

D MAJOR

3. Place a T after the statements which are true; an F after the ones which are false.
   F a) All triads are major.
   T b) A triad is a chord with three notes.
   T c) The notes of the triad are called the root, the third, and the fifth.
   F d) The triad on the first degree of the scale is called the dominant triad.
   T e) From the root to the third of a major triad is a major third.
   T f) The most important chords in any key are the tonic and the dominant.
   F g) If a triad is built on each degree of the major scale, only two of them are major.
4. Indicate with a semibreve the Home Note of each of these major key signatures.

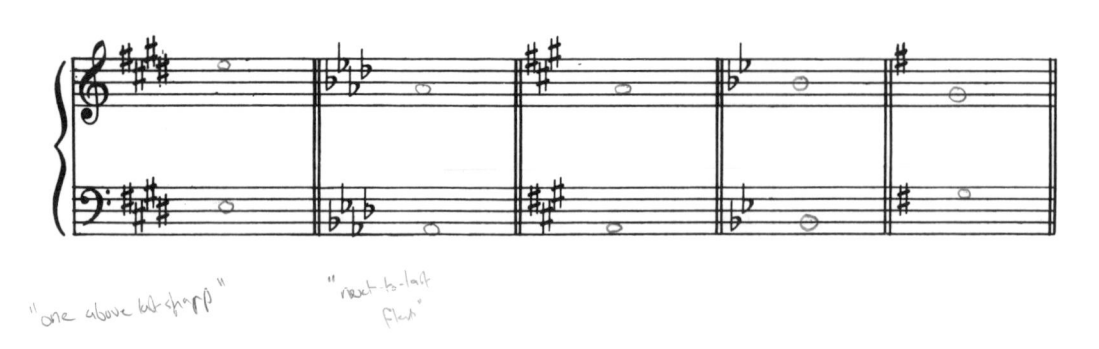

"one above last sharp"   "next-to-last flat"

LESSON 14
HARMONISING MELODIES

Many melodies can be harmonised using only the Tonic and Dominant triads. In order to give you an opportunity to use your knowledge of chords, here are some folk songs to play.

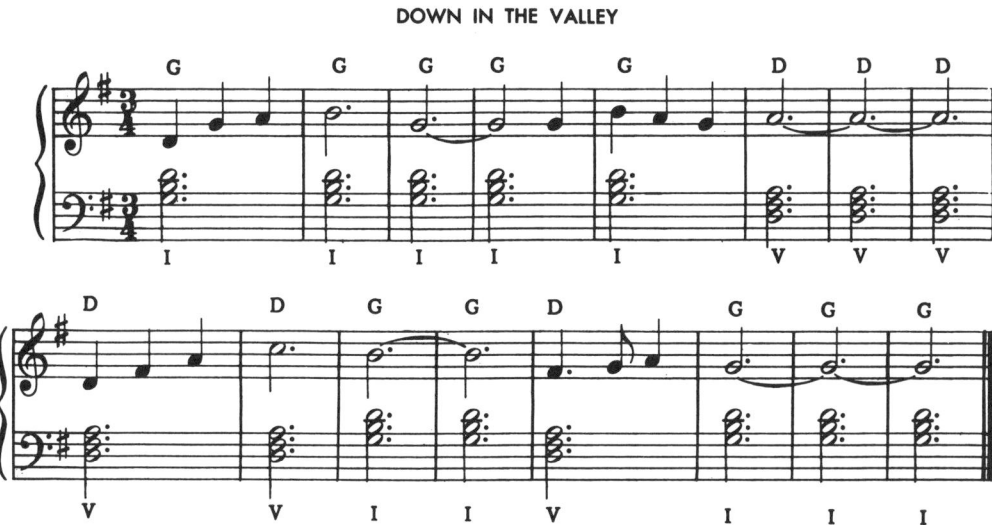

DOWN IN THE VALLEY

Playing the chords in this way does not give a very polished accompaniment. But as you learn more about chords, you will be able to improve the left hand parts. Even now, however, you can see chords in action.

In the remaining examples, the left hand part is not written in. Instead, you will find the letter name of the triad you are to play. C indicates a C Major triad, F an F Major triad. The Roman numerals have also been written in to indicate whether the chord is tonic or dominant. Write in the triads at first; but with practice, this should not be necessary.

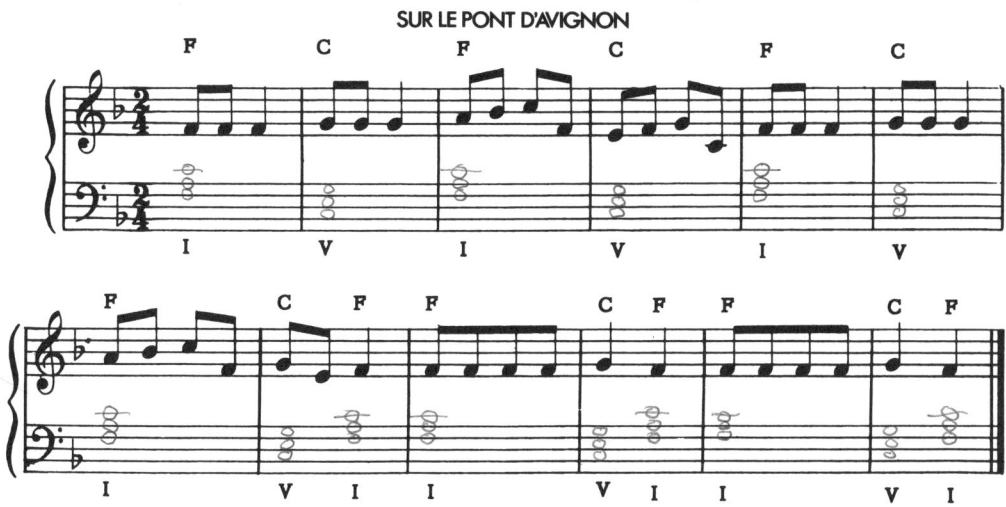

SUR LE PONT D'AVIGNON

WORK SHEET 14

Write in the chords for these folk tunes. Then learn to play them correctly.

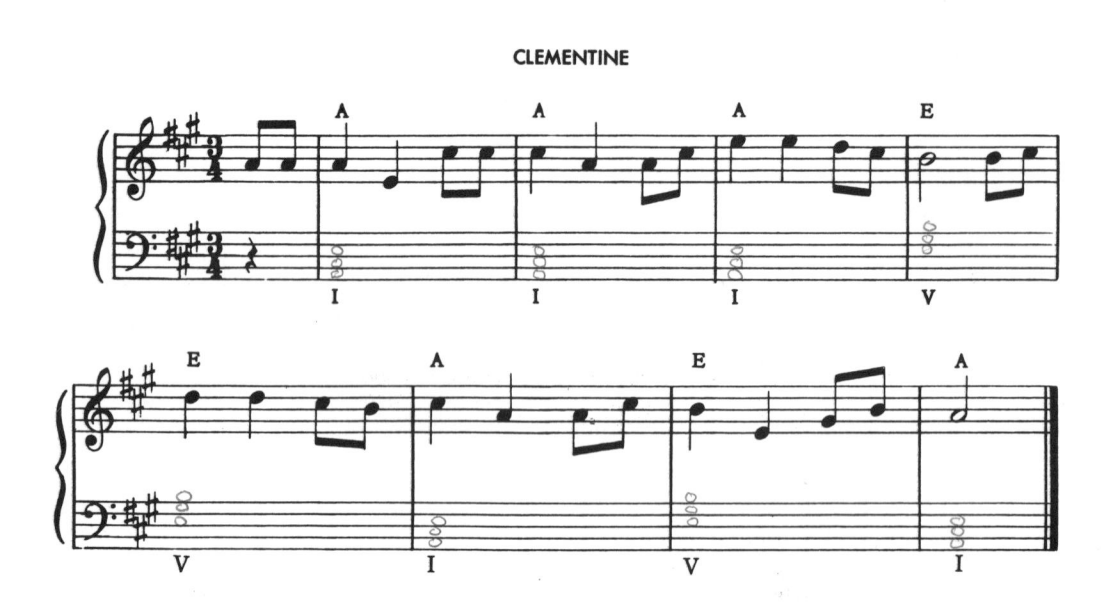

CLEMENTINE

HERE, RATTLER, HERE

LESSON 15
REVIEW WORK SHEET

1. Write the major scale pattern. t t s t t t s
2. Write the following major scales. Write the scale degrees and mark the semitones with slurs.

   D MAJOR

   B♭ MAJOR

   G MAJOR

   E♭ MAJOR

3. Write in the beats for these examples. Use "ands" where necessary.

4. Mark the true statements T; the false ones F.

   F a) $\frac{6}{8}$ time is the same as $\frac{3}{4}$ time.

   T b) The triad on the first degree of the scale is called the tonic triad.

   F c) Any major triad takes its name from the name of its root.

   F d) The key signature of E Major has four flats.

   T e) It is possible to start a major scale on any note.

LESSON 15
REVIEW WORK SHEET (Continued)

5. Write the following key signatures. Indicate the Key Note.

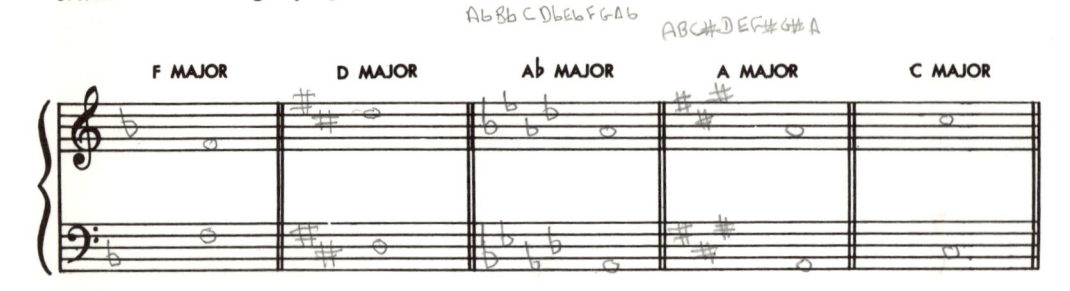

Ab Bb C Db Eb F G Ab   A B C# D E F# G# A

F MAJOR   D MAJOR   Ab MAJOR   A MAJOR   C MAJOR

6. Identify these intervals. Where you know the exact name, be sure to use it.

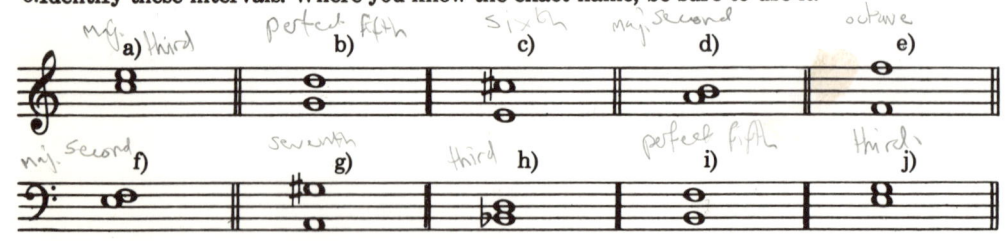

a) maj third   b) perfect fifth   c) sixth   d) maj second   e) octave

f) maj second   g) seventh   h) third   i) perfect fifth   j) third

7. Write the tonic and dominant triads in the keys indicated by these key signatures.

I

8. Fill in the blanks.
a) A major second is a ...tone...

b) There are ...7... semitones in a perfect fifth. A ...chromatic... scale is made up of semitones only.
c) One crotchet note equals ...4... semiquavers.
d) The chord on the fifth step of the scale is called the ...dominant...
e) Lines added above or below the staff are called ...ledger... lines.
f) The scale of A Major has ...3... sharps.
g) A chord where the notes are played one after another is called a ...broken... chord.

PART THREE
LESSON 1
A REVIEW OF INTERVALS – MINOR THIRDS

An interval is the distance between two notes. We measure intervals by counting the number of letters involved including the names of the two notes making up the interval. From A up to D is a fourth because there are four letter names involved — A, B, C, and D. In PART TWO you learned the number names of all intervals (seconds, thirds, fourths, etc.)

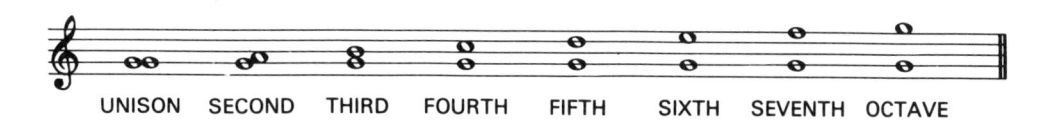

UNISON   SECOND   THIRD   FOURTH   FIFTH   SIXTH   SEVENTH   OCTAVE

To distinguish between different intervals with the same number of letter names - from C to D or from C to D flat - it is necessary to count the number of semitones. We have already learned the following exact names of intervals: Minor Second - one semitone; Major Second - two semitones; Major Third - four semitones; Perfect Fifth - seven semitones. We now add: Perfect Unison (or Prime) - same note, no semitones; Perfect Octave - twelve semitones.

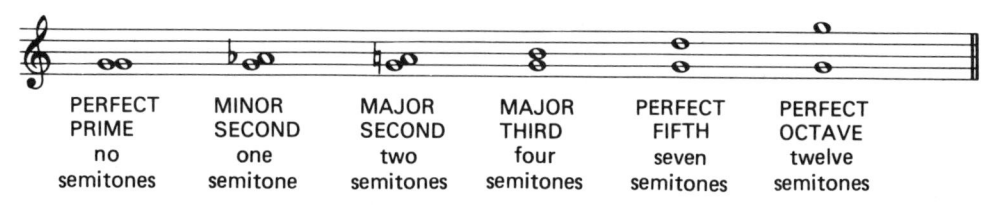

PERFECT PRIME — no semitones
MINOR SECOND — one semitone
MAJOR SECOND — two semitones
MAJOR THIRD — four semitones
PERFECT FIFTH — seven semitones
PERFECT OCTAVE — twelve semitones

Since the words Major and Minor mean larger and smaller, it is easy to change a major interval into a minor one. Simply lower the upper note one semitone. A major second has two semitones while a minor second has only one. In the same way, a major third has four semitones and a minor third only three:

Maj. 3rd   Min. 3rd   Maj. 3rd   Min. 3rd   Maj. 3rd   Min. 3rd   Maj. 3rd   Min. 3rd

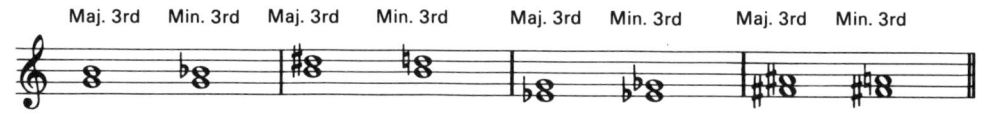

In order to be a minor third, however, there must be three different letter names involved. From E to G is a minor third because there are three semitones and three letter names (E, F, and G). From E flat to G flat is also a minor third. But from E flat to F sharp is not a minor third because, although there are three semitones, there are only two letter names — E and F.

Min. 3rd   Min. 3rd   2nd

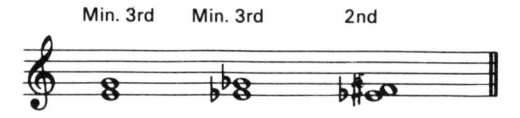

WORK SHEET 1

1. Identify the following intervals. Use the exact name when you know it.

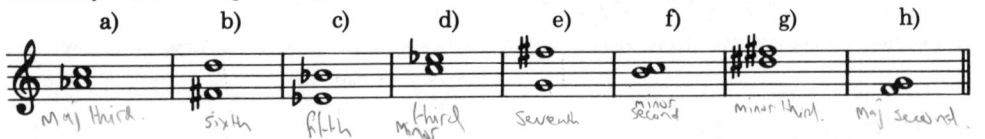

a) Maj third   b) sixth   c) fifth   d) minor third   e) seventh   f) minor second   g) minor third   h) Maj second

2. Mark these intervals as major thirds or minor thirds. Cross out any other intervals.

major third, minor third, [crossed out], minor third, [crossed out], major third, major third

3. Change these major thirds into minor thirds.

4. Build a minor third on each of these notes.

5. How many semitones are there in each of the following intervals?

    a) Major second __2__
    b) Minor third __3__
    c) Perfect octave __12__

    d) Perfect fifth __7__
    e) Minor second __1__
    f) Major third __4__

6. Write the note the correct interval above each of these notes.

PERFECT FIFTH   MINOR THIRD   SIXTH   MAJOR SECOND   PERFECT OCTAVE   FOURTH   MAJOR THIRD

LESSON 2
MINOR TRIADS

A major triad is made up of a root, a major third, and a perfect fifth. A Minor Triad is made up of a root, a *minor third,* and a perfect fifth. It is easy to change a major triad into a minor triad. Simply change the major third into a minor third by lowering it one semitone. Keep the same letter name.

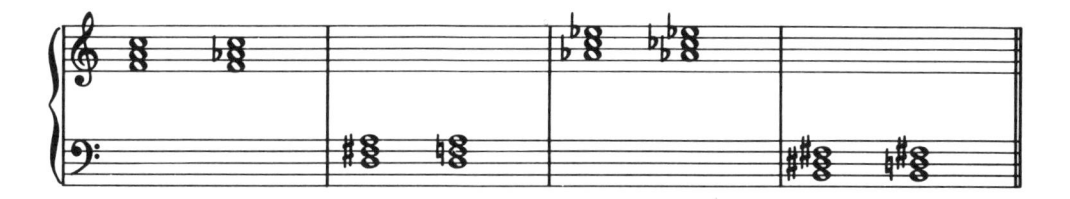

If we now build a white-key triad on each note of the C Major scale, we will have an opportunity to study major and minor triads.

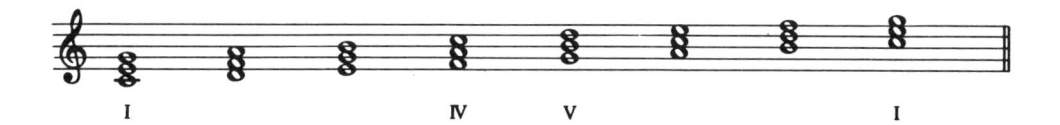

We have already seen that the triads on I, IV, and V are all major triads, and in PART TWO you harmonized melodies using tonic (I) and dominant (V) triads. We can see from the example above that three of the other triads are minor: the ones on the second, third, and sixth degrees of the scale.

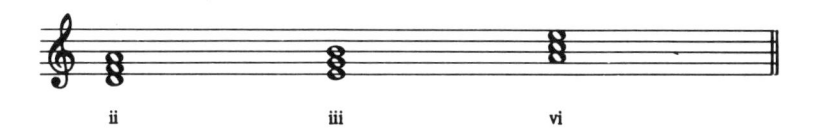

The Roman numerals used to represent minor triads are usually made with lower case letters instead of the capital letters we use for major triads. Thus, these minor triads will be designated ii, iii, and vi.

WORK SHEET 2

1. Which triads are major and which are minor?

a) Minor b) Major c) minor d) minor e) Major f) minor g) Major

2. Change these major triads into minor triads.

3. Change these minor triads into major triads.

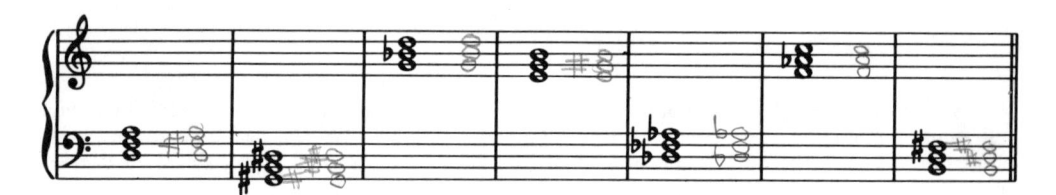

4. Build a minor triad on each of these notes.

LESSON 3
HARMONISING MELODIES USING MINOR TRIADS

So far, you have harmonised folk tunes using only tonic (I) and dominant (V) triads. Now that you have studied minor triads and learned how to form them, you can also use them in harmonising melodies in major keys. As you saw in the last lesson, the triads on the second, third, and sixth degrees of the major scale are minor triads. Of these three, the ones on ii and vi are the ones most frequently used.

For the chord symbols which we shall put above the melody line, we will use Gm, and Dm to indicate G minor, and D minor triads, since that is the way you will find them written in popular music. However, you should also know that g and d are sometimes used to indicate minor triads.

Here is an example of a folk song using both major and minor triads in its harmonies. Be sure to practise finding and playing the chords before trying to play the two hands together.

POLISH FOLK TUNE

WORK SHEET 3

Here are two folk songs with minor triads included in their harmonies. Write in all the chords indicated by the chord symbols.

Cornish

Dutch

LESSON 4
MINOR SCALES AND THE MINOR SCALE OUTLINE

There is only one form of the major scale, but there are several different kinds of minor scales. We will start our study of minor scales by learning how they are alike. In all forms of the minor scale, the scale degrees 1, 2, 3, 4, 5, and 8 are always the same. Let us call this the *Minor Scale Outline*. It is only the scale degrees 6 and 7 which change and distinguish one form of the minor scale from another.

If we compare the notes of the minor scale outline with the corresponding notes of the major scale, we find that the only difference is that the third note of the minor scale outlines is one semitone lower, just as the third of the minor triad was one semitone lower than the third of the major triad. In fact, we may think of filling in the notes around the minor triad to form the minor scale outline.

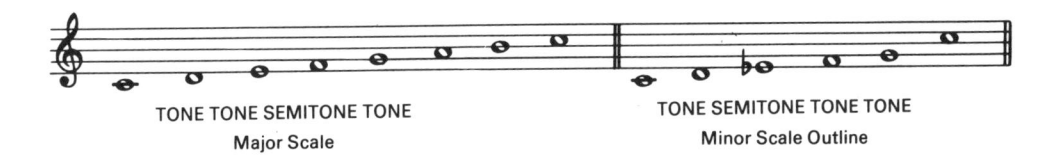

TONE TONE SEMITONE TONE
Major Scale

TONE SEMITONE TONE TONE
Minor Scale Outline

As you can see, the semitone comes between 2 and 3 in the minor scale outline, while it comes between 3 and 4 in the major scale.

If you try to fill in the sixth and seventh scale degrees at the piano, you will find that there are five possibilities: A natural-B natural, A flat-B flat, A flat-B natural, A natural-B flat, and A sharp-B natural. Play the scale using each of these pairs of notes to fill in the sixth and seventh degrees going up and down. Which ones sound best to you? In music, the first, second, and third pairs are the ones we meet most frequently, the fourth less often, and the fifth almost never.

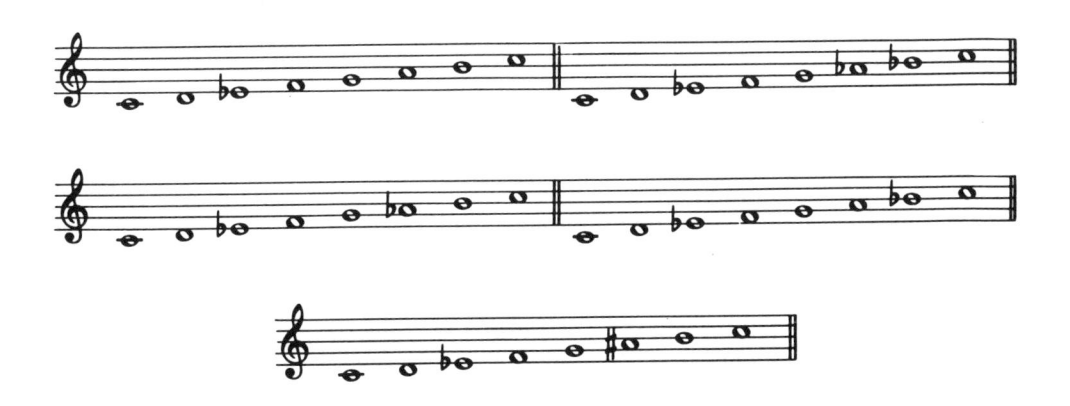

71

WORK SHEET 4

1. a) Write the pattern of the first five scale degrees of the major scale. T T S T

   b) Write the pattern of the first five scale degrees of the minor scale. T S T T

2. Change these examples from major to minor. Play them on the piano.

3. Write the scale outline of the following minor scales. Play them on the piano.

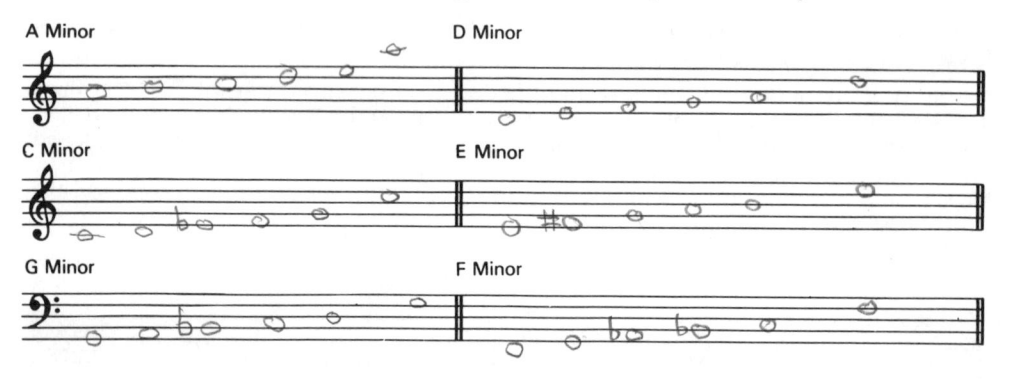

   A Minor

   D Minor

   C Minor

   E Minor

   G Minor

   F Minor

4. Write in the beats for the following examples, then clap the rhythms.

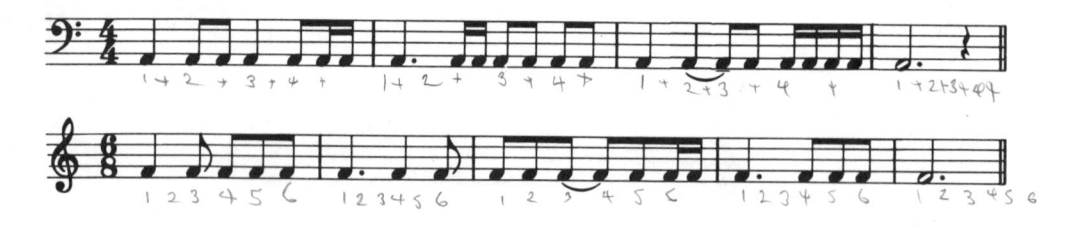

   1 + 2 + 3 + 4 +   1 + 2 + 3 + 4 +   1 + 2 + 3 + 4 +   1 + 2 + 3 + 4 +

   1 2 3 4 5 6   1 2 3 4 5 6   1 2 3 4 5 6   1 2 3 4 5 6   1 2 3 4 5 6

LESSON 5
THE ASCENDING MELODIC MINOR SCALE

Now that you have learned the minor scale outline — those notes of the minor scale which are the same in all forms — we can start to learn how to fill in the sixth and seventh degrees correctly to form the different varieties of minor scales. Remember it is only the sixth and seventh degrees which distinguish one form of the minor scale from another.

Let us start out by using a tone from 5 to 6 and a tone from 6 to 7. That will leave a semitone from 7 to 8.

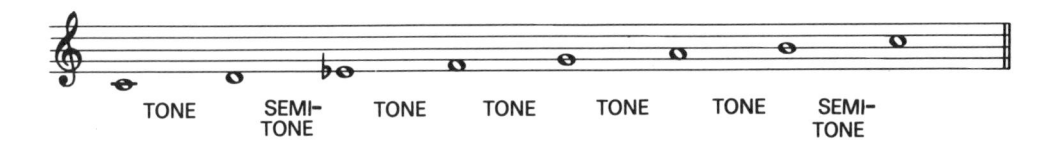

| TONE | SEMI-TONE | TONE | TONE | TONE | TONE | SEMI-TONE |

Now compare that to the parallel major scale pattern:

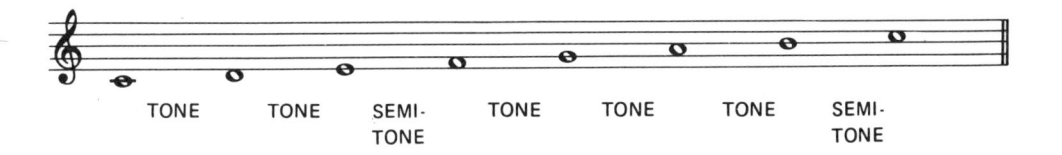

| TONE | TONE | SEMI-TONE | TONE | TONE | TONE | SEMI-TONE |

You can see that the only difference is that the semitone which comes between 3 and 4 in the major scale comes between 2 and 3 in this form of the minor scale.

The tones between 5 and 6 and 6 and 7 and the semitone between 7 and 8 make this scale move up very smoothly. For that reason, it is called the ASCENDING MELODIC MINOR SCALE. The word *ascending* means "going up," and you will almost always find this form of the minor scale going up.

The ascending melodic minor scale on C has only an E Flat. But when you studied the correct order of flats in PART TWO, you learned that the first flat is always B Flat. So at this time we will have to write the ascending melodic minor scale without using a key signature. Simply write in the sharps or flats needed to make up the correct pattern of tones and semitones.

WORK SHEET 5

1. Change the following major scales into ascending melodic minor scales.

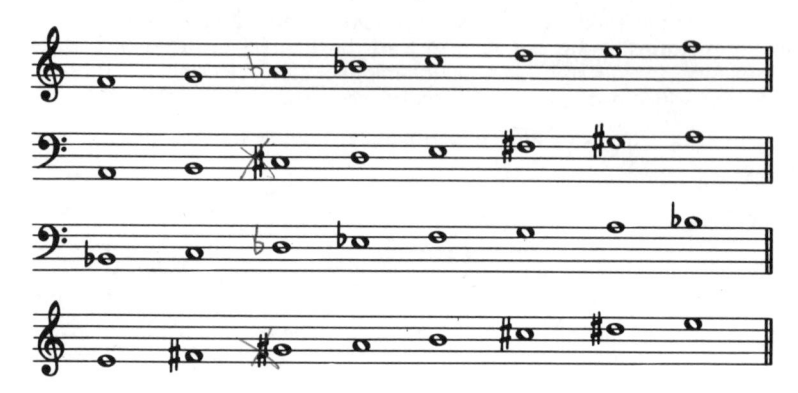

2. Fill in the sixth and seventh scale degrees in these minor scale outlines to form correct ascending melodic minor scales.

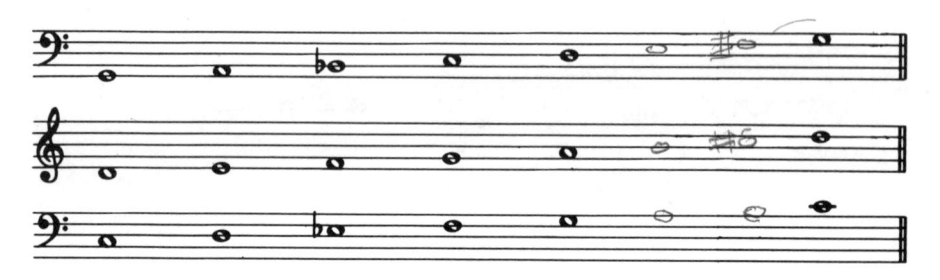

3. Change these minor thirds into major thirds.

4. Write the major scale indicated by each of these key signatures. Then make the necessary alteration to change it into the parallel ascending melodic minor scale.

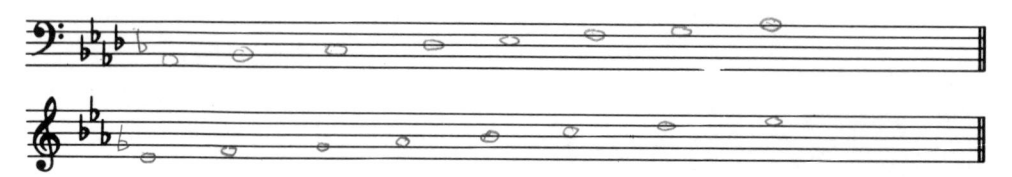

LESSON 6
NATURAL MINOR SCALES AND MINOR KEY SIGNATURES

In Lesson 5 we used the pattern TONE TONE SEMITONE for the upper tetrachord of a minor scale, just like the upper tetrachord of the major scale. But we found that the notes of the Ascending Melodic Minor Scale did not correspond to the pattern of flats and sharps used in key signatures. Now let us try some scales following the pattern SEMITONE TONE TONE for the upper tetrachord.

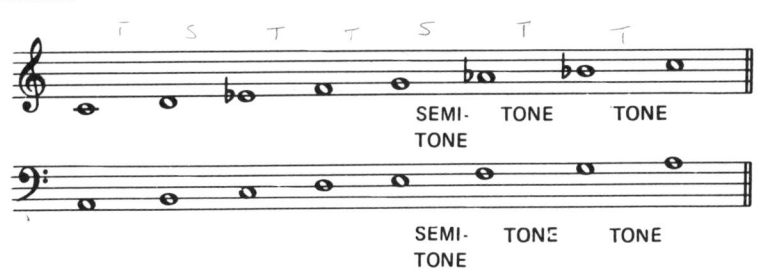

Notice that the scale starting on C has E flat, A flat, and B flat. Is there any key signature which uses those flats? Did you notice that the scale on A has no sharps or flats, just like C major? When a major and a minor scale use the same key signature, we speak of them as RELATIVES: C minor is the relative minor of E flat major; A minor is the relative minor of C major. The relative minor is always found on the sixth degree of the major scale. (We can also find the relative minor by counting down three semitones from the tonic of the relative major).

RELATIVE MAJOR   RELATIVE MINOR

This form of the minor scale, using only the notes of the key signature with no alterations, is called the NATURAL MINOR SCALE. There are not many familiar melodies based on this scale, but "God Rest Ye, Merry Gentlemen" is one. Most melodies use the pattern we learned for the ascending melodic minor scale when they are going up and this form when coming down. For that reason, the Natural Minor Scale is also known as the Descending Melodic Minor Scale.

It will be easy to remember which form of the melodic minor scale has the raised sixth and seventh degrees and which the lowered if you simply think that when going up we raise them and when coming down we lower them. That is, in C minor we use A natural and B natural going up and A flat and B flat coming down. We can see this clearly in this C Melodic Minor Scale.

REMEMBER: Raise — Up; Lower — Down

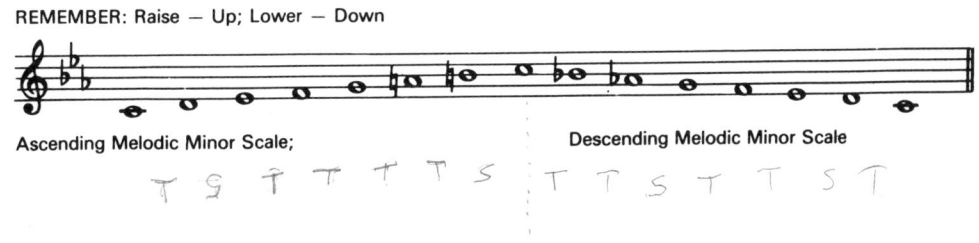

Ascending Melodic Minor Scale;   Descending Melodic Minor Scale

WORK SHEET 6

1. Change these major scales into descending melodic minor scales by lowering the third, sixth, and seventh degrees one semitone each.

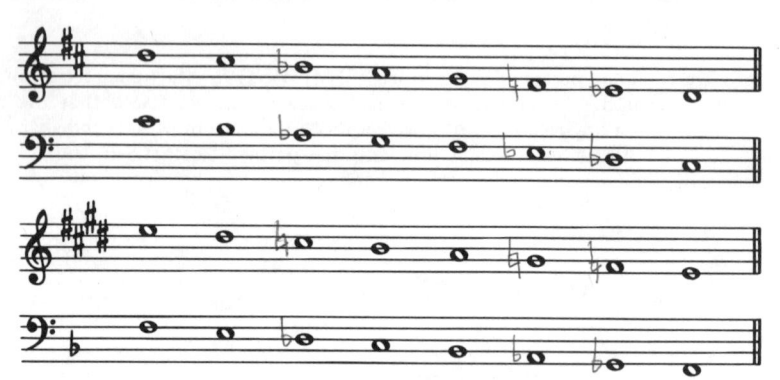

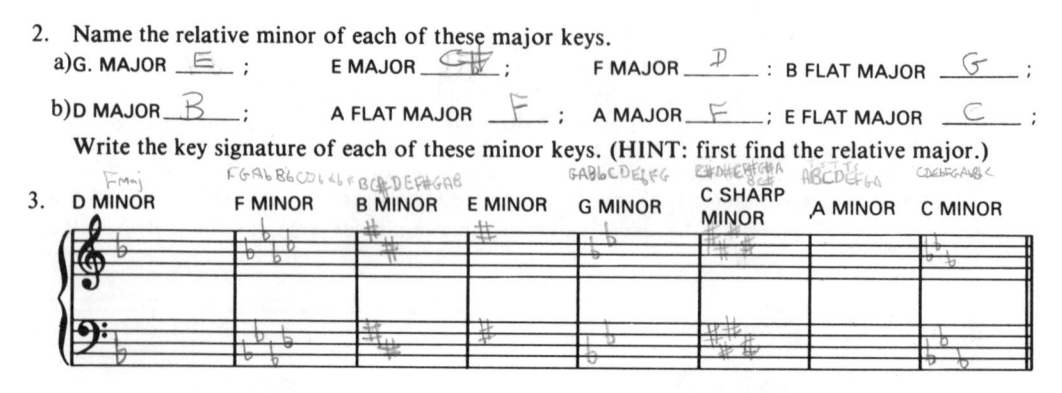

2. Name the relative minor of each of these major keys.
   a) G. MAJOR __E__ ;   E MAJOR __C#__ ;   F MAJOR __D__ ;   B FLAT MAJOR __G__ ;
   b) D MAJOR __B__ ;   A FLAT MAJOR __F__ ;   A MAJOR __F#__ ;   E FLAT MAJOR __C__ ;

   Write the key signature of each of these minor keys. (HINT: first find the relative major.)

3. D MINOR   F MINOR   B MINOR   E MINOR   G MINOR   C SHARP MINOR   A MINOR   C MINOR

4. Write the descending melodic minor scale indicated by each of these key signatures.

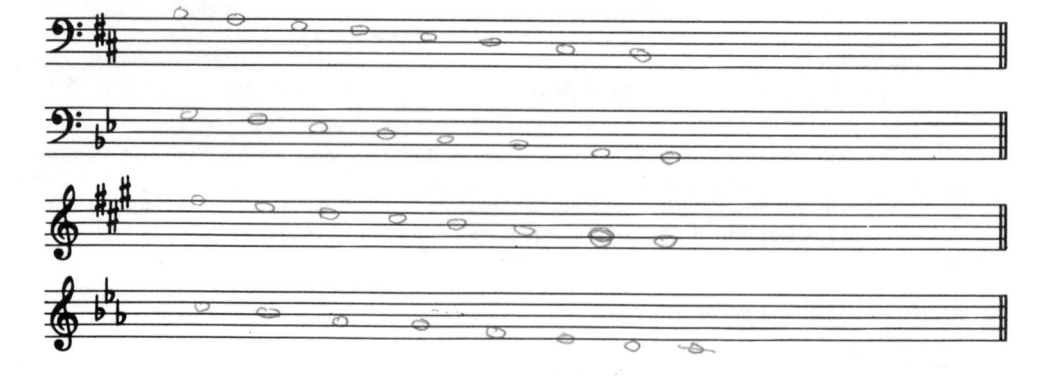

LESSON 7
PIANO-STYLE ACCOMPANIMENTS

It is not difficult to change the simple chords you have been playing into piano style accompaniments. All you have to do is find a way of spreading the notes of the chord out over the whole bar instead of playing them all together on the first beat. Here are some common patterns in different kinds of time.

Of course, the possibilities are unlimited, and you can use more elaborate forms as your skill increases. Try this Czech Folk Song, first playing the chords on the first beat of the bar, then with the accompaniment written in, and finally using some of the figures given above. Try to decide which sounds best.

When you can do this, go back and try playing good piano style accompaniments for some of the other melodies you have harmonised. In general, it should not be necessary to change any of the harmonies. But occasionally, the form of the accompaniment figure will make harmony changes on individual notes difficult or impossible to play. Then it may become necessary to leave out one chord. Be on the lookout for interesting accompaniment patterns in the pieces you study.

WORK SHEET 7

1. Write a good piano style accompaniment for this folk song.

German

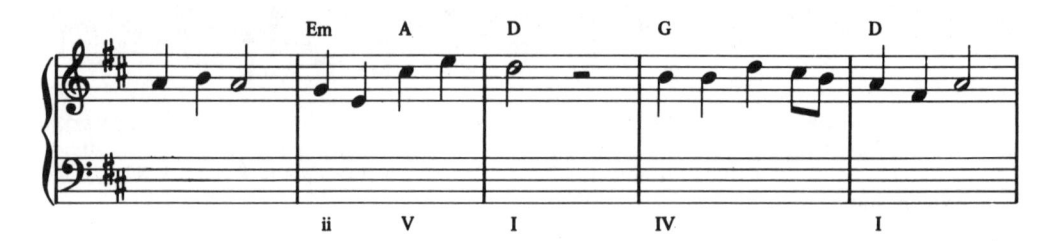

2. Draw a line to connect the words or phrases in the left-hand column with the ones they match in the right-hand column.

    ascending melodic minor scale   root, minor third, perfect fifth
    minor triad   lowered sixth and seventh degrees
    use the same key signature   minor third
    major triad   relative major and minor
    four semitones   root, major third, perfect fifth
    descending melodic minor scale   major third
    characteristic interval of minor scales and triads   raised sixth and seventh degrees

3. Write a G melodic minor scale, ascending and descending.

LESSON 8
HARMONISING MINOR KEY MELODIES

With the knowledge of major and minor triads which you already have, it is possible to harmonize some simple melodies in minor keys. We will not investigate the qualities of the chords on the different degrees of the minor scale at this time. Simply follow the indications for major and minor triads. As in the past, play the melody first with a chord accompaniment; then try it with a good piano style accompaniment.

IRISH FOLK TUNE

A suggestion for one possible form of accompaniment is given in the first bar. In bar 3, where the melody has the note C of the F minor triad, the suggested accompaniment figure has only F and A flat. We could play all three notes in the left hand if we moved the chord down an octave, but then it would sound too deep. If you practise regularly at working out accompaniments to melodies, many different ways of solving the problems will come up. Harmonising melodies in this way is only meant for folk tunes and popular songs and not for the works of the great composers. As your knowledge of theory increases, you will be able to supply better and more polished accompaniments. At this time, you are just getting practice in using your knowledge of major and minor triads.

WORK SHEET 8

Here are two folk songs in minor keys for you to harmonise. Work out your own accompaniment.

JOSHUA FIT DE BATTLE OF JERICHO

British Navy Song

LESSON 9
THE HARMONIC MINOR SCALE

The third and last form of the minor scale is called the *Harmonic Minor Scale*. As its name implies, it is the form which determines the qualities of the various chords, whether they are major, minor, or otherwise. We might also say that the notes of this scale come from the notes of the principal chords. In the folk tune in C minor which you harmonized in Lesson 8, the tonic triad was made up of the notes C, E flat, and G; the iv chord or subdominant was made up of the notes F, A flat, and C; and the dominant was made up of the notes G, B, and D.

C E flat G	F A flat C	G B D
i	iv	v

Or, arranged in alphabetical order, as all scales must be,

C D E flat F G A flat B C

These are the notes of the harmonic minor scale. Its notes are the same whether we play it going up or coming down. We still have semitones between two and three and between seven and eight, but we also have a semitone between five and six which leaves 3 semitones between six and seven.

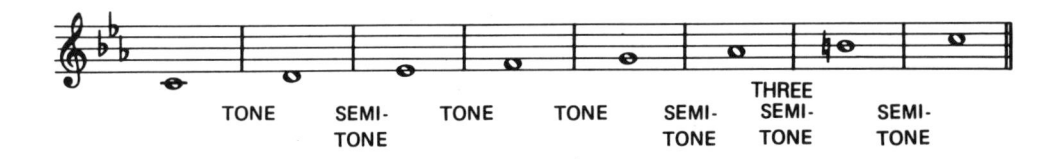

| TONE | SEMI-TONE | TONE | TONE | SEMI-TONE | THREE SEMI-TONE | SEMI-TONE |

Since the key signature of C minor has three flats, B flat, E flat, and A flat, and the Harmonic Minor Scale has B natural, it will be seen that in writing this scale, we must add the natural to the seventh degree. In all harmonic minor scales, the seventh degree must be raised one semitone. This supplies the major third for the dominant triad.

Now let us compare the qualities of the principal chords in major and minor keys.

	IN MAJOR	IN MINOR
I (TONIC)	MAJOR	MINOR
IV (SUBDOMINANT)	MAJOR	MINOR
V (DOMINANT)	MAJOR	MAJOR

In major keys, tonic, subdominant, and dominant are all major. In minor keys, tonic and subdominant are minor, but the dominant is major.

REMEMBER: The dominant is almost always major whether we are in major or minor.

WORK SHEET 9

1. Are the following triads major or minor?
   a) Tonic triad in major ___Maj___
   b) Dominant triad in minor ___Maj___
   c) Subdominant triad in minor ___Min___
   d) Subdominant triad in major ___Maj___
   e) Tonic triad in minor ___Min___
   f) Dominant triad in major ___Maj___

2. When the key signature is given, which degree of the minor scale is changed in order to form the harmonic minor scale? ___seventh___
   Is it raised or lowered? ___raised___
   Why is it changed? ___to make dominant triad major___

3. Write the harmonic minor scale indicated by these key signatures.

4. Write the following harmonic minor scales, first putting in the key signature of each.

   E MINOR

   D MINOR

   A MINOR

LESSON 10
TRIPLETS

So far, you have learned to divide a crotchet into two quavers or four semiquavers. But sometimes a composer may want to divide a note into three equal parts. Such a group is called a TRIPLET and must be indicated by a sign ⌐―3―⌐. A crotchet equals two quavers or a triplet of quavers.

When a piece is made up of a mixture of triplets and true quavers, the triplets should all be marked with the triplet sign. Here is an example.

If a whole piece is made up of triplets, the composer usually indicates only the first few. After that, he will expect you to understand that the others are the same.

Other notes beside the crotchet may be divided into triplets. Any three equal notes played in the time normally taken by two form a triplet. A minim equals a triplet of crotchets; a quaver note equals a triplet of semiquavers.

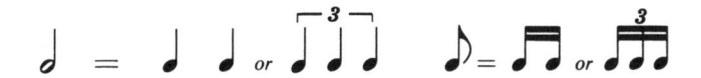

In order to decide what kind of note is equal to a given triplet, simply think of what kind of note would be equal to two notes of the same value as the notes of the triplet. On the other hand, if you are writing and wish to use a triplet, think of dividing the note into two parts, and that will be the same kind of note value you should write for your triplet.

WORK SHEET 10

1. Write one note equal in value to each of the triplets. Write a triplet equal in value to each of the single notes.

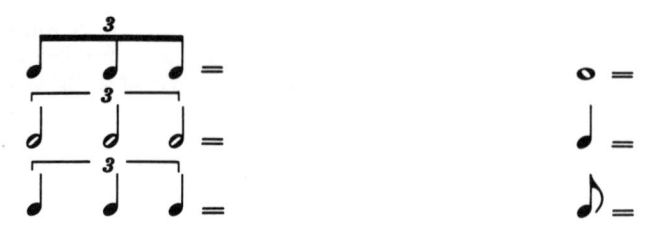

2. Write in the beats for these bars.

3. Write the following key signatures.

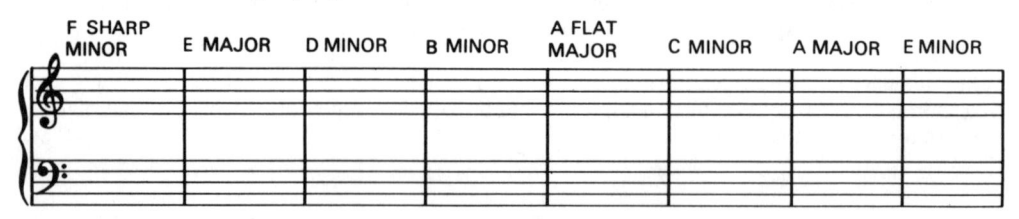

   F SHARP MINOR   E MAJOR   D MINOR   B MINOR   A FLAT MAJOR   C MINOR   A MAJOR   E MINOR

4. Write the E melodic minor scale, ascending and descending.

5. Identify these intervals, using the exact name wherever you know it.
   a) b) c) d) e) f) g)

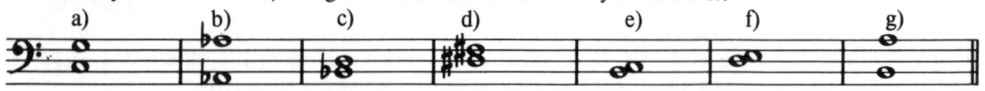

* an alternative way of writing $\frac{4}{4}$

LESSON 11
EXACT NAMES OF ALL MAJOR, MINOR, AND PERFECT INTERVALS

You have already learned to identify the number names of all intervals and the exact names of major and minor seconds, major and minor thirds, and perfect unisons, fifths, and octaves. Now it is time to learn the exact names of the remaining major, minor, and perfect intervals: major and minor sixths and sevenths and perfect fourths.

From the tonic to the fourth note of the scale, whether major or minor, is a perfect fourth. How many semitones are there in a perfect fourth? (Hint: count the semitones from C to F.)

PERFECT FOURTH: Five Semitones

From the tonic to the sixth note of the major scale is a major sixth. Since the words major and minor mean larger and smaller, all we need do to form a minor sixth is to lower the upper note of a major sixth one semitone.

MAJOR SIXTH: Nine Semitones   MINOR SIXTH: Eight Semitones

Similarly, from the tonic to the seventh note of the major scale is a major seventh. That makes eleven semitones, one less than an octave. The minor seventh is one semitone smaller and has ten semitones, two semitones less than an octave.

MAJOR SEVENTH: Eleven Semitones (one less than an octave)   MINOR SEVENTH: Ten Semitones (two less than an octave)

IMPORTANT: Unisons, fourths, fifths, and octaves are the only intervals which can be perfect. They are the same in all forms of the major and minor scales. Seconds, thirds, sixths, and sevenths may be either major or minor. From the tonic to the second, third, sixth, or seventh notes of the major scale make a major second, third, sixth, or seventh. The minor interval is always one semitone smaller than the major.

WORK SHEET 11

1. How many Semitones are there in each of the following intervals?

   a) perfect fifth _____   g) minor sixth _____
   b) major seventh _____   h) perfect fourth _____
   c) minor third _____   i) minor seventh _____
   d) major second _____   j) perfect unison _____
   e) perfect octave _____   k) major sixth _____
   f) major third _____   l) minor second _____

2. Identify each of these intervals. Use the exact name where you know it.

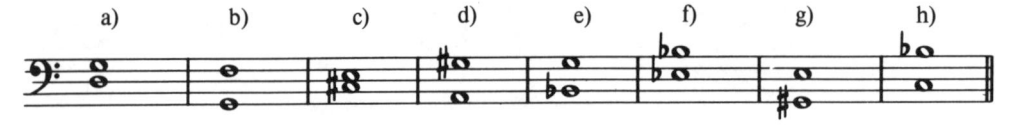

3. Form the intervals called for above these notes.

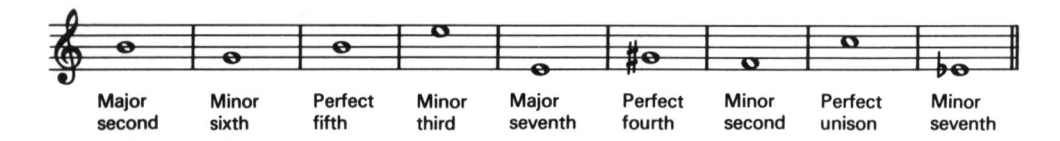

   Major second | Minor sixth | Perfect fifth | Minor third | Major seventh | Perfect fourth | Minor second | Perfect unison | Minor seventh

4. Write in the beats for these examples using only the numbers. Then clap them.

LESSON 12
THE DOMINANT SEVENTH CHORD

Not all chords are triads. Some have four or even more different notes. The most common of these chords is the DOMINANT SEVENTH CHORD. As you might guess from its name, it is built on the dominant, the fifth degree of the scale. It is formed by adding to the dominant triad a note a minor seventh above the root (or three semitones above the fifth of the triad).

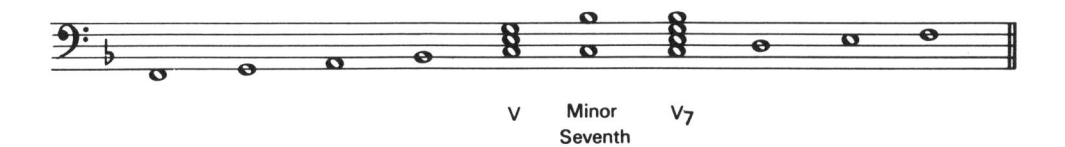

You should practise playing dominant seventh chords on the piano. Start by playing minor sevenths on each note of the chromatic scale. Remember that a minor seventh is a whole step less than an octave. Practise playing minor sevenths until you have the sound in your ear and the feel in your hand. When you have done this, build a major triad on each note of the chromatic scale and add to it the note a minor seventh above the root (as shown in the example above).

Like the dominant triad, the dominant seventh chord is the same in both major and minor. Its chord symbol is V_7 (or G7, F7, or D7, etc. depending on the root). It is very important to think of the dominant seventh chord in relation to the key of which it is the dominant. If you think of a dominant seventh chord on G (a G7 chord), you must remember it is not in the key of G. It is in the key of C (major or minor), since G is the dominant of C.

To help you think of the dominant seventh chord in relation to its key, play all the major and minor scales you know, stopping on the fifth degree to build a dominant seventh chord. Be sure to practise doing this with both hands. You may start out following the example above, but as you develop more skill, you may be able to form the dominant seventh chord without first forming the triad and the seventh separately.

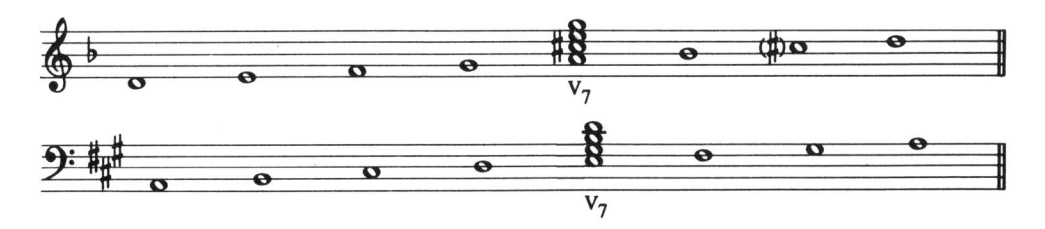

Look for dominant seventh chords in your pieces.

VERY IMPORTANT: The chord symbol V_7 indicates a chord with a seventh built on the dominant. The Roman numeral V indicates the scale degree, while the Arabic 7 indicates that the chord contains the interval of a seventh.

WORK SHEET 12

1. Circle the minor sevenths.

2. Form a dominant seventh chord on each of these notes.

3. Write the dominant seventh chord in each of these keys.

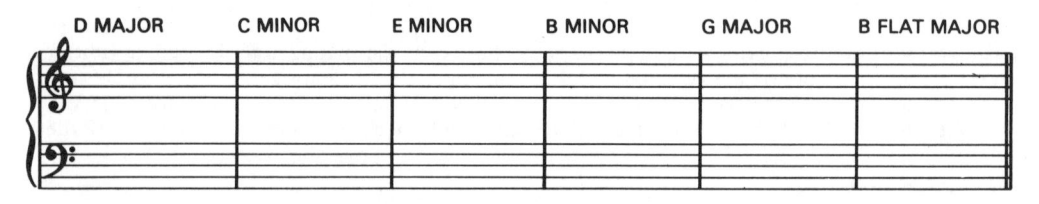

   D MAJOR   C MINOR   E MINOR   B MINOR   G MAJOR   B FLAT MAJOR

4. Write the D harmonic minor scale, ascending and descending, using the key signature. Build a dominant seventh chord on the fifth degree.

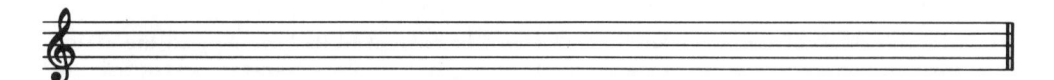

Write the B melodic minor scale, ascending and descending, using the key signature. Build a dominant seventh chord on the fifth degree.

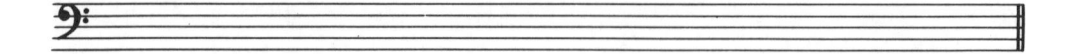

5. Here are some key signatures. Write the names of the major keys they indicate above and the minor keys below.

LESSON 13
USING THE DOMINANT SEVENTH CHORD

In pieces, the dominant seventh chord will usually be followed by a tonic triad. Most pieces end with the chords V7 — I (or V — I). These chords can also be used to mark the end of a section of a piece. In music, an ending figure of this sort is called a CADENCE. There are many different kinds of cadences, but the most important is the Perfect cadence, which consists of the chords V7 — I (or V — I). In order to get the sound of this cadence in your ear and the feel of it in your hands, you should practise playing dominant seventh chords in as many keys as possible, following each with its tonic triad. Generally, in this progression, the fifth is left out of the tonic triad. But you should practise playing the cadence both ways. Don't forget the minor keys!

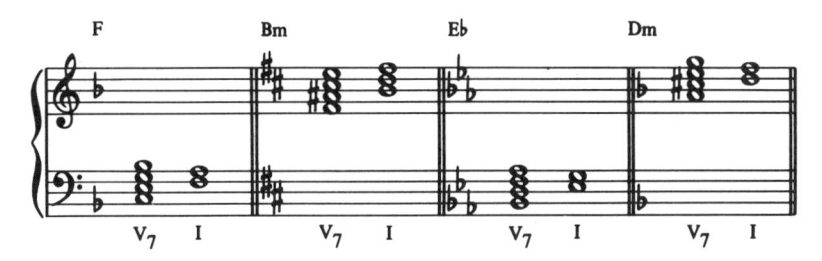

Because the dominant seventh chord has four different tones, it may sometimes present difficulties for piano style accompaniments. Sometimes one of the notes is omitted — most frequently the fifth. Here are a few solutions and suggestions for piano style dominant seventh chords.

It is impossible to give a rule which tells you when to use a dominant triad and when to use a dominant seventh chord. Your ear must tell you. Go back to the melodies you have already harmonised and substitute a dominant seventh chord for each dominant triad. Listen very carefully and try to decide which sounds better. It is only through this kind of listening and experimenting that you will develop real skill at harmonising melodies at the piano.

Check the endings of the pieces you are playing to look for perfect cadences. Listen for the difference between V — I and V7 — I.

WORK SHEET 13

1. Name the key of which each of the following chords is the dominant seventh.

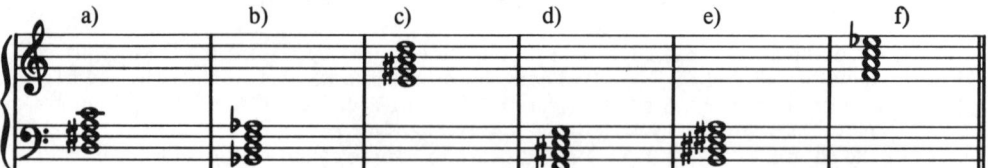

   a)   b)   c)   d)   e)   f)

2. After writing the dominant seventh chord of the following keys, follow it with a tonic triad. Put the fifth in some of the tonic triads and leave it out of the others.

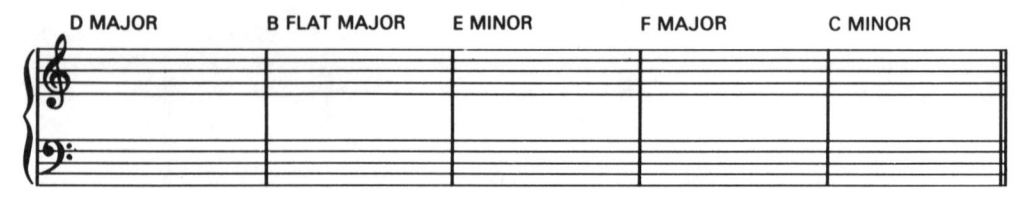

   D MAJOR   B FLAT MAJOR   E MINOR   F MAJOR   C MINOR

3. Here is a melody to harmonise. Supply a good piano style accompaniment. Be careful to use a dominant triad and not a dominant seventh chord in bar 12.

   GERMAN FOLK SONG

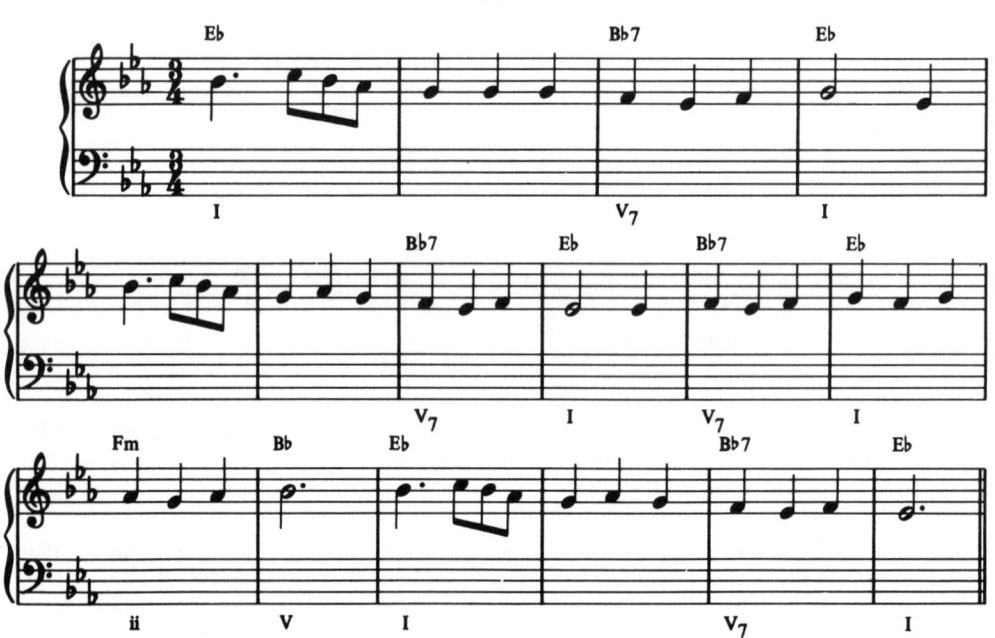

LESSON 14
SUMMARY OF MINOR SCALES AND TRIADS

There are two different ways of relating minor keys to major keys. If we think of major and minor keys starting on the same tone, we speak of *Parallel* major and minor keys: C major and C minor; E major and E minor. If we think of the major and minor keys using the same key signature, we speak of *Relative* major and minor keys: C major and A minor; F major and D minor.

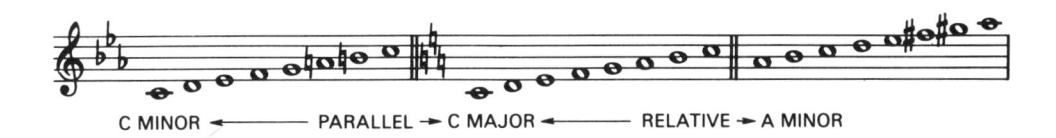

C MINOR ← ─── PARALLEL → C MAJOR ← ─── RELATIVE → A MINOR

The minor third is the characteristic interval of minor scales and triads. It is the only difference between the major triad and the minor triad. And if we think about the minor scale in relation to the parallel major, this minor third is the only note changed to form the ascending melodic minor scale.

D MAJOR   D MINOR   D MAJOR SCALE   D ASCENDING MELODIC MINOR SCALE

In learning the minor scales, it is helpful to remember that the three forms differ from one another only in the sixth and seventh degrees. The other notes of these scales are always alike. Just think of the minor key outline, which consists of those notes of the scale which do not change.

ASCENDING MELODIC   DESCENDING MELODIC

HARMONIC

In the ascending melodic minor, the sixth and seventh degrees are raised because we are going up and that helps us move up more smoothly; descending, the sixth and seventh degrees are lowered to help us move down more smoothly. This descending form of the scale uses the notes of the minor key signature and is, therefore, called the natural minor. In the harmonic minor scale, the seventh is raised so that the dominant triad will be major.

WORK SHEET 14

1. Which degrees are the same in all forms of the minor scale? _____.
2. Here is a minor scale outline. Write underneath the names of the notes needed to make it a melodic minor scale (ascending and descending.) Next, write the names of the notes required to make it a harmonic minor scale (ascending and descending.)

Melodic minor _____ and _____; harmonic minor _____ and _____.

3. Here are some triads. Change the major ones to minor and the minor ones to major.

4. Write the following scales. Use the correct minor key signature.

    A HARMONIC MINOR

    C SHARP ASCENDING MELODIC MINOR

    G MELODIC MINOR (Ascending and Descending)

    F NATURAL MINOR

    D HARMONIC MINOR

LESSON 15
REVIEW WORK SHEET

1. How many forms of the minor scale are there in common use?_____

   Name them. _____

   In the ascending melodic minor scale are the sixth and seventh degrees raised or lowered?

   _____.

2. a) What is the relative minor of each of the following major keys? D major_____;

   E major_____;   E flat major_____;   A major_____.

   b) Name the relative major of each of the following minor keys. G minor_____;

   A minor_____;   F minor_____;   E minor_____;   B flat minor_____.

   c) Give the parallel major or minor of the following keys. G major_____;

   D minor_____;   B flat major_____;   F sharp major_____.

3. Write the key signatures of these keys.

   B MINOR   C SHARP MINOR   B FLAT MAJOR   E MAJOR   G MINOR   A FLAT MAJOR   F SHARP MINOR

4. Write the following chords.

   F MINOR   E FLAT 7   D FLAT MAJOR   G SHARP MINOR   C7   B FLAT MAJOR   A7

5. Write in the counts for these examples.

* an alternative way of writing $\frac{4}{4}$

LESSON 15
REVIEW WORK SHEET (Continued)

6. Write the dominant seventh chord and tonic triad indicated by each of these major key signatures.

7. Resolve each of these dominant seventh chords to its tonic minor.

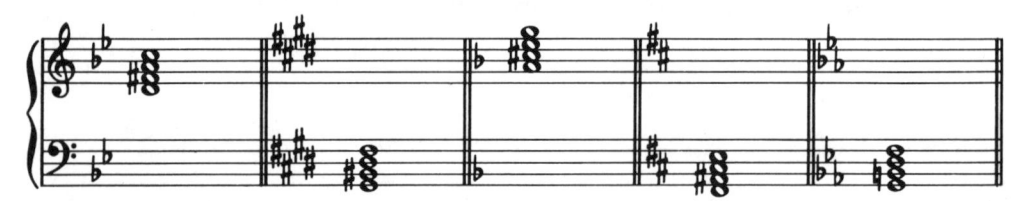

8. Write the following scales. Use correct key signatures.

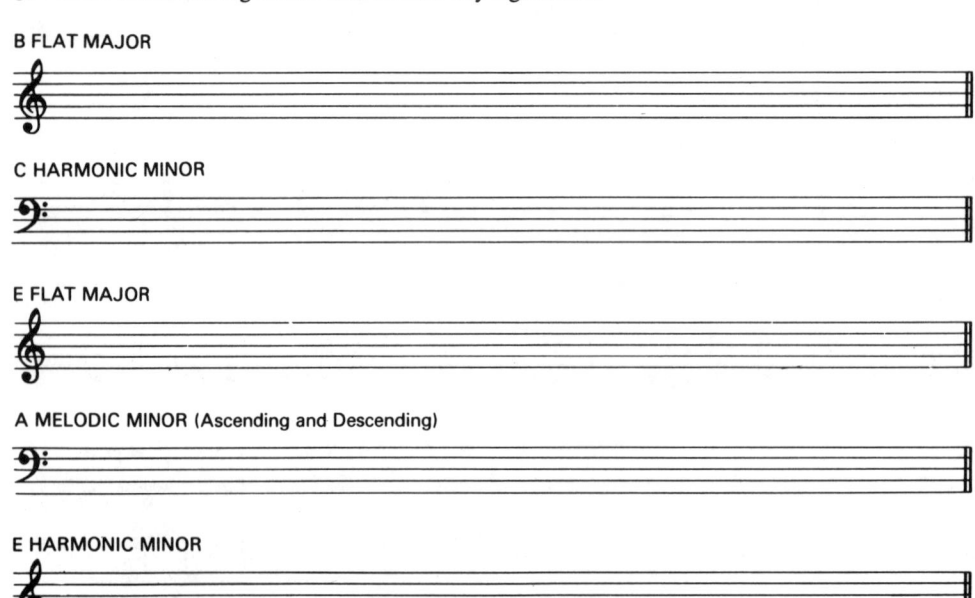

B FLAT MAJOR

C HARMONIC MINOR

E FLAT MAJOR

A MELODIC MINOR (Ascending and Descending)

E HARMONIC MINOR

THEORY BOOK ANSWERS

UNDERSTANDING MUSIC THEORY

PART ONE

WORK SHEET 1 (p. 6)

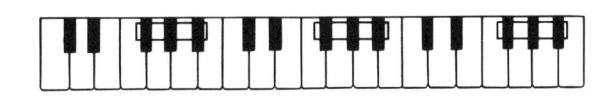

1. [keyboard diagram with groups of two black keys circled]

2. [keyboard diagram with groups of three black keys marked]

3. E F G A B C D

4. G F E D C B A

5. ABC DEF BCD FGA EFG GAB CDE

6. [keyboard labelled G D G D G D]

7. [keyboard labelled D G C E A D F C]

WORK SHEET 2 (p. 8)

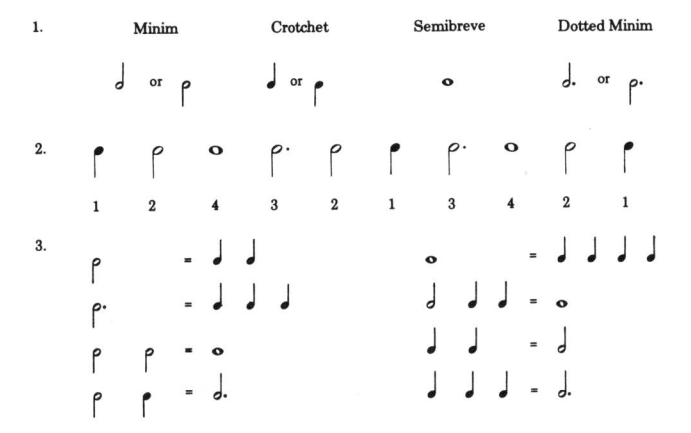

1.
Minim	Crotchet	Semibreve	Dotted Minim
𝅗𝅥 or 𝄽	♩ or 𝄽	𝅝	𝅗𝅥. or 𝄽.

2. ♩ ♩ 𝅝 ♩. ♩ ♩ ♩. 𝅝 ♩ ♩

   1 2 4 3 2 1 3 4 2 1

3.
- ♩ = ♪ ♪
- ♩. = ♪ ♪ ♪
- ♩ ♩ = 𝅝
- ♩ ♩ = ♩.

- 𝅝 = ♪ ♪ ♪ ♪
- 𝅗𝅥 𝅗𝅥 = 𝅝
- 𝅗𝅥 𝅗𝅥 = 𝅗𝅥
- 𝅗𝅥 𝅗𝅥 𝅗𝅥 = 𝅗𝅥.

4.

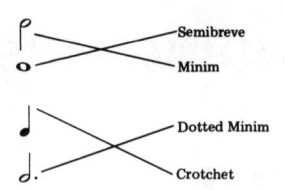

- 𝅗𝅥 — Semibreve
- 𝅝 — Minim
- 𝅘𝅥 — Dotted Minim
- 𝅘𝅥. — Crotchet

5.

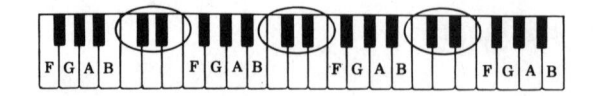

WORK SHEET 3 (p. 10)

1.

2.

3.

WORK SHEET 4 (p. 12)

1.

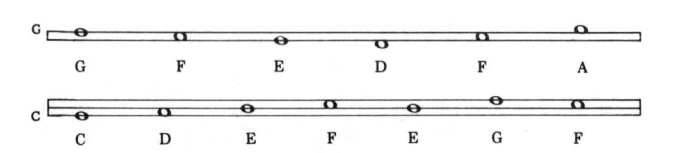

G F E D F A

C D E F E G F

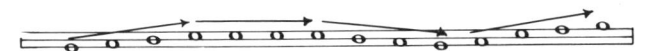

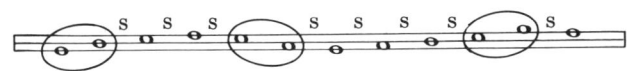

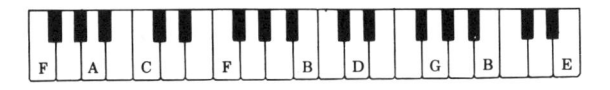

WORK SHEET 5 (p. 14)

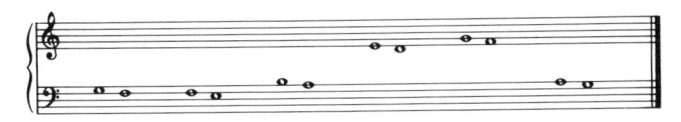

4. E, MIDDLE C, G, B, D, F

WORK SHEET 6 (p. 16)

1.

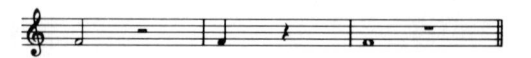

2. 2, 3, 1, 2, 1, 4, 3, 4, 2, 1

3.

4.

5. BED; EGG; BAG; CAB

WORK SHEET 7 (p. 18)

1. C, G, D, G, E, C, B

2. FADE; CAGE; BEEF

3. FEED   AGED   BEAD   CAFE

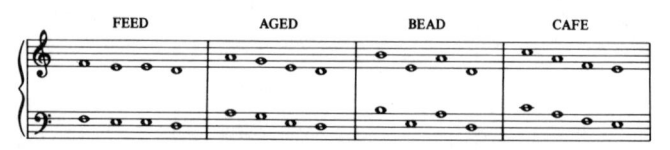

4.

WORK SHEET 8 (p. 20)

1. F Sharp   G Sharp   C Sharp   A Sharp   C Sharp   D Sharp

C Sharp   F Sharp   B Sharp   G Sharp   D Sharp   F Sharp

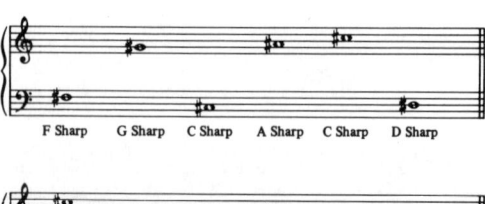

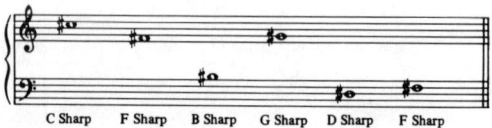

3.

4.

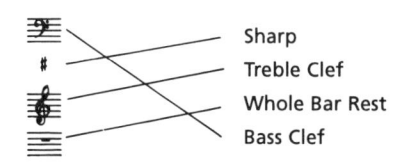

- Sharp
- Treble Clef
- Whole Bar Rest
- Bass Clef

WORK SHEET 9 (p. 22)

1.

B Flat   E Flat   G Flat   A Flat   E Flat   D Flat

2.

3.

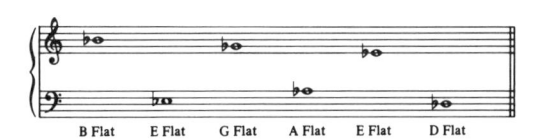

4. 1, 1, 2, 4, 2, 1, 3, 4, 1

5.

WORK SHEET 10 (p. 24)

1. ♪ or ; ᶅ ; ♫ or

2.

1 + 2 + 3 + 4 +   1 + 2 + 3 + 4 +   1 + 2 + 3 + 4 +   1 + 2 + 3 + 4 +

1 + 2 + 3 +   1 + 2 + 3 +   1 + 2 + 3 +   1 + 2 + 3 +

3.

4.

5.

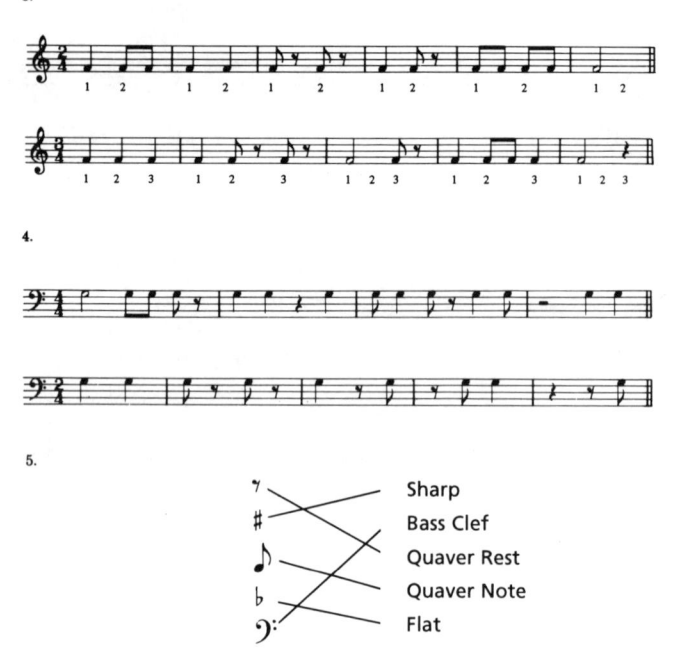

♩ ——————— Sharp
♯ ——————— Bass Clef
♪ ——————— Quaver Rest
♭ ——————— Quaver Note
𝄢 ——————— Flat

WORK SHEET 11 (p. 26)

1.

2.

3.

4.   F
    F
    F (A Semibreve Rest can signify one whole bar's rest, regardless of how many beats in the bar)
    T

5.   EDGE   FADED   GAB   CEDE

WORK SHEET 12 (p. 28)

1.

2.

3.

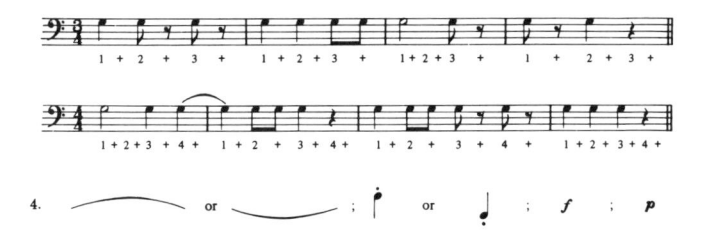

4.

WORK SHEET 13 (p. 30)

1.

2. ADDED; CABBAGE; FACE

3. $\frac{3}{4}$; $\frac{4}{4}$

WORK SHEET 14 (p. 32)

1.

2. Soft; Connected; Separated; Loud

3.

REVIEW WORK SHEET (pp. 33,34)

1. CAGED; DEAF; BAGGAGE

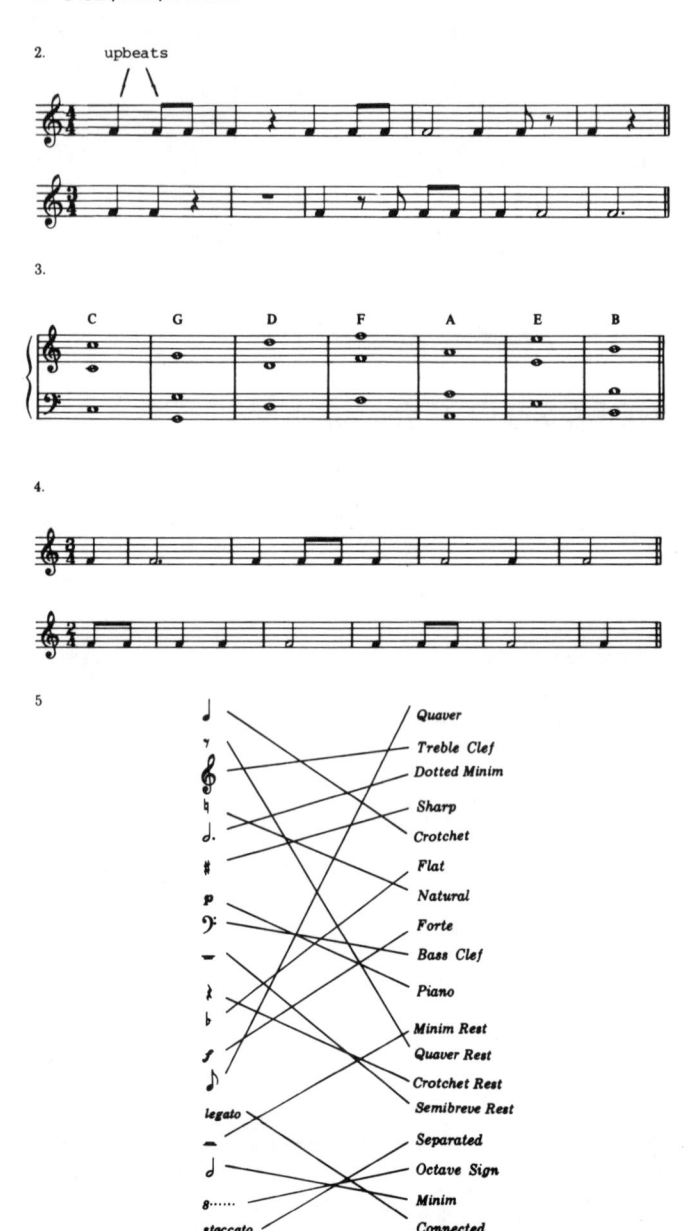

2. upbeats

3.

    C   G   D   F   A   E   B

4.

5.

- Quaver
- Treble Clef
- Dotted Minim
- Sharp
- Crotchet
- Flat
- Natural
- Forte
- Bass Clef
- Piano
- Minim Rest
- Quaver Rest
- Crotchet Rest
- Semibreve Rest
- Separated
- Octave Sign
- Minim
- Connected

PART TWO

WORK SHEET 1 (p. 36)

1.

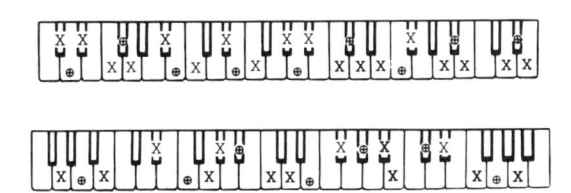

2.

3. a) G♭ G♯, E♭ F, B C♯, A♭ A♯, C D, E F♯, A B
   b) G B, C E, D F♯, F♯ A♯, A♭ C, E♭ G, B E♭
   c) The white key semitones fall between B and C, and between E and F
   d) The black key tones come between F♯ and G♯, between G♯ and A♯, and between C♯ and D♯. (or between G♭ and A♭, between A♭ and B♭, and between D♭ and E♭)

4.

WORK SHEET 2 (p. 38)

1. F G A B C; E D C B A G; A B C D E F; G F E D C

2. CAGED; FACE; BABE; DEAF

3.

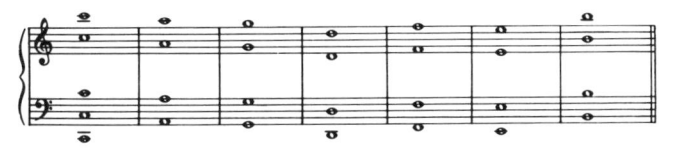

4.

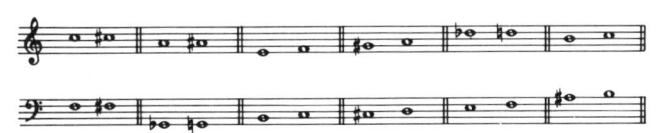

WORK SHEET 3 (p. 40)

1. a) In music, a SCALE is a succession of notes starting from any note and moving by step to the note an octave higher (or lower).

    b) E and F; B and C

    c) TONE TONE SEMITONE TONE TONE TONE SEMITONE

    d) KEY NOTE, HOME NOTE, TONIC

    e) The major scale (and any other scale) gets its name from the note on which we start the pattern.

2.

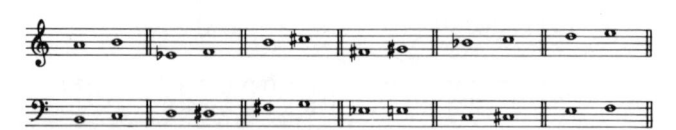

3.

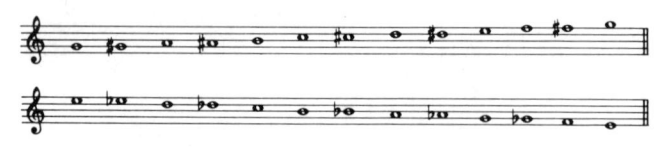

4.

WORK SHEET 4 (p.42)

1. a) 1,2,3,4,5,6,7,8

    b) TWO

    c) TONE TONE SEMITONE

    d) TONE TONE SEMITONE

    e) One Tone

    (f) 1   2   3   4   5   6   7   8
        TONE TONE SEMI- TONE TONE TONE SEMI-
                    TONE   TONE

2.

3. CAFE; BEGGED; ADAGE; AGE

WORK SHEET 5 (p. 44)

1.

2.
   D MAJOR

   G MAJOR

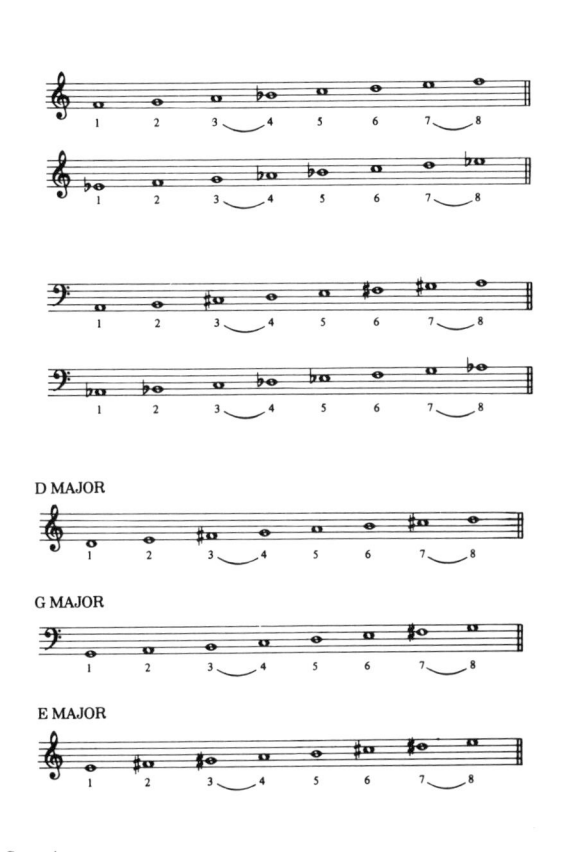

   E MAJOR

3. a) C   A
   b) F♯   C♯
   c) E   D
   d) G   A

WORK SHEET 6 (p. 46)

1.

2.

3.

A MAJOR

E♭ MAJOR

4.

WORK SHEET 7 (p. 48)

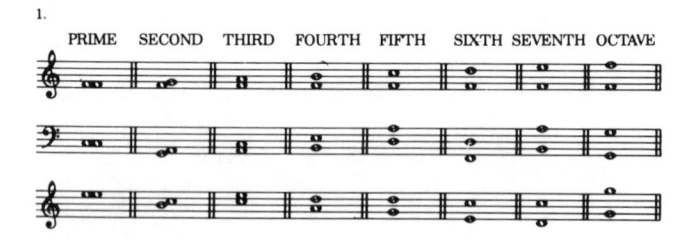

1.

PRIME SECOND THIRD FOURTH FIFTH SIXTH SEVENTH OCTAVE

2. a) THIRD, FIFTH OCTAVE, FOURTH, SEVENTH, FIFTH, SIXTH
   b) SECOND, OCTAVE, THIRD, SIXTH, FOURTH, SEVENTH, FIFTH
   c) TONE TONE SEMITONE TONE TONE TONE SEMITONE

3. BEADED, EGAD, FACADE, EDGE

WORK SHEET 8 (p.50)

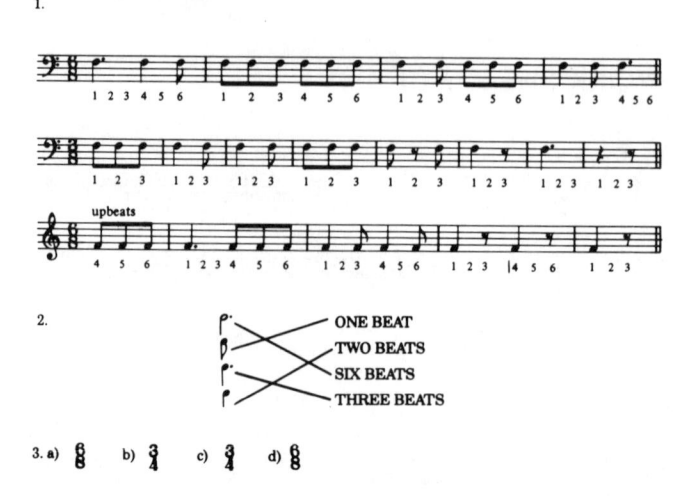

1.

2. ♩· ——— ONE BEAT
    ♩ ——— TWO BEATS
    ♩· ——— SIX BEATS
    ♩ ——— THREE BEATS

3. a) 6/8   b) 3/4   c) 3/4   d) 6/8

4. THIRD, OCTAVE, FIFTH, SECOND, FOURTH, SEVENTH, SIXTH

WORK SHEET 9 (p. 52)

1. F#, C#, G#, D# ; B♭, E♭, A♭, D♭

2.

3. a) F#   b) B♭, E♭   c) F#, C#, G#   d) B♭   e) F#, C#, G#, D#   f) F#, C#
   g) B♭, E♭, A♭, D♭   h) B♭, E♭, A♭.

4. C# E♭ D B G# E♭ A♭ B

WORK SHEET 10 (p.54)

1. a) D F A C E G B
   b) A CHORD is several notes played at one time.
   c) A TRIAD is a chord made up of three notes arranged in thirds.
   d) FIRST, THIRD, and FIFTH

2.

3.

4.

5.

WORK SHEET 11 (p. 56)

1. a) ONE, SEVEN, FOUR, TWO
   b) LARGER, SMALLER

2.

3.

4. MAJOR THIRD; MINOR SECOND; PERFECT FIFTH;
   MAJOR SECOND; PERFECT FIFTH

5.

WORK SHEET 12 (p. 58)

1.

2.

3.

4.

WORK SHEET 13 (p. 60)

1. a) TONIC TRIAD   b) DOMINANT TRIAD

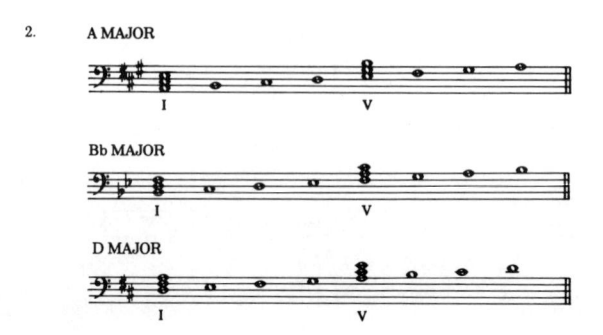

2. A MAJOR

   Bb MAJOR

   D MAJOR

3. a) F b) F c) T d) F e) T f) T g) F

4.

SUR LE PONT D'AVIGNON (p. 61)

WORK SHEET 14 (p. 62)

CLEMENTINE

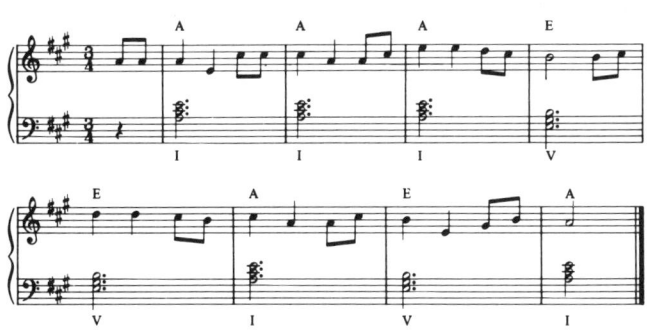

HERE, RATTLER, HERE

REVIEW WORK SHEET (p. 63)

1. TONE TONE SEMITONE TONE TONE TONE SEMITONE

2. D MAJOR

   B♭ MAJOR

   G MAJOR

   E♭ MAJOR

3.

4. a) F b) T c) T d) F e) T

5.

6. a) MAJOR THIRD   f) MINOR SECOND
   b) PERFECT FIFTH   g) SEVENTH
   c) SIXTH   h) MAJOR THIRD
   d) MAJOR SECOND   i) FIFTH
   e) OCTAVE   j) THIRD

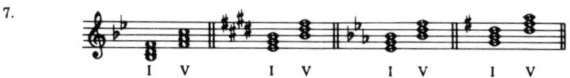

7.

8. a) TONE   e) LEGER (or LEDGER)
   b) SEVEN; CHROMATIC   f) THREE
   c) FOUR   g) BROKEN
   d) DOMINANT

PART THREE

WORK SHEET 1 (p. 66)

1. a) MAJOR THIRD e) SEVENTH
   b) SIXTH f) MINOR SECOND
   c) PERFECT FIFTH g) MINOR THIRD
   d) MINOR THIRD h) MAJOR SECOND

2. MAJOR THIRD, MINOR THIRD, MINOR THIRD, MAJOR THIRD, MAJOR THIRD

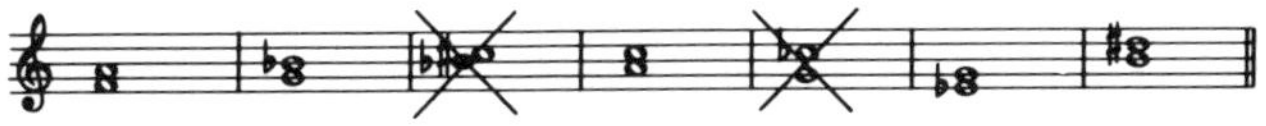

3.

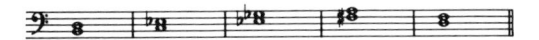

4.

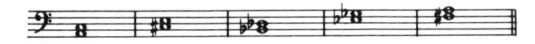

5. a) TWO d) SEVEN
   b) THREE e) ONE
   c) TWELVE f) FOUR

6. PERFECT FIFTH, MINOR THIRD, SIXTH, MAJOR SECOND, PERFECT OCTAVE, FOURTH, MAJOR THIRD

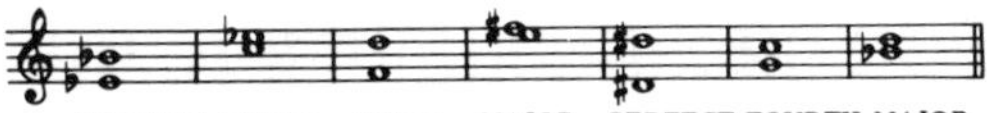

WORK SHEET 2 (p.68)

1. a) MINOR e) MAJOR
   b) MAJOR f) MINOR
   c) MINOR g) MAJOR
   d) MINOR

2.

3.

4.

POLISH FOLK TUNE (p. 69)

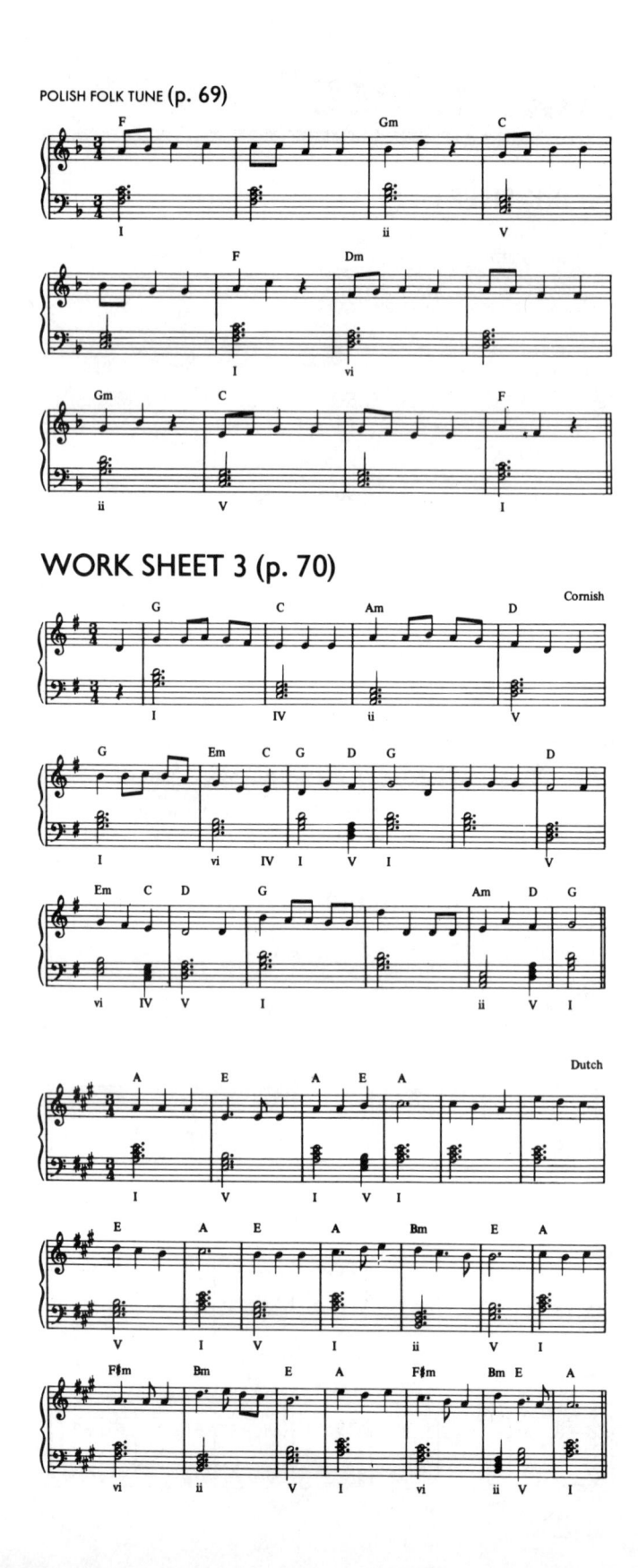

WORK SHEET 3 (p. 70)

WORK SHEET 4 (p. 72)

1. a) TONE TONE SEMITONE TONE
   b) TONE SEMITONE TONE TONE

2.

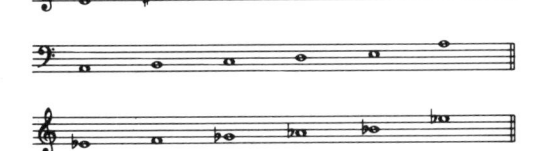

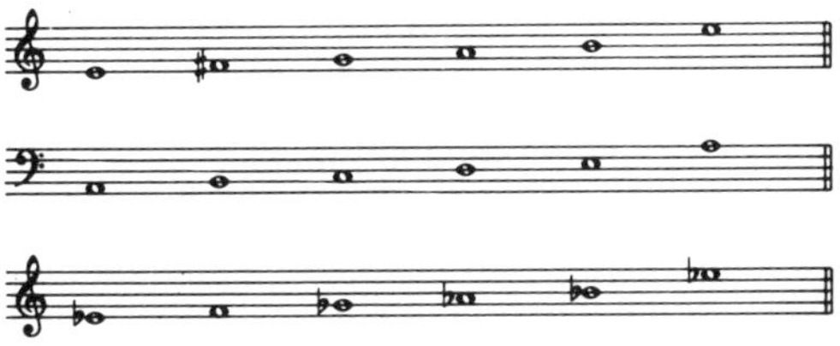

3.
   A MINOR   D MINOR
   C MINOR   E MINOR
   G MINOR   F MINOR

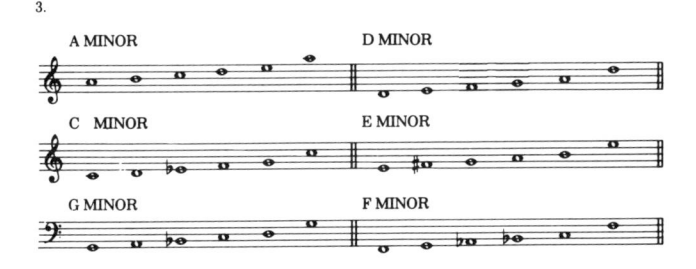

4.

WORK SHEET 5 (p. 74)

1.

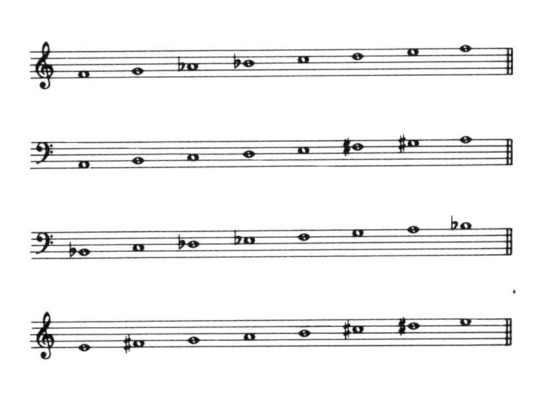

2.

3.

4.

WORK SHEET 6 (p. 76)

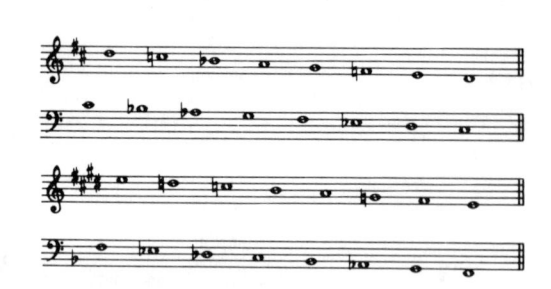

1.

2. a) E MINOR; C# MINOR; D MINOR; G MINOR
   b) B MINOR; F MINOR; F# MINOR; C MINOR

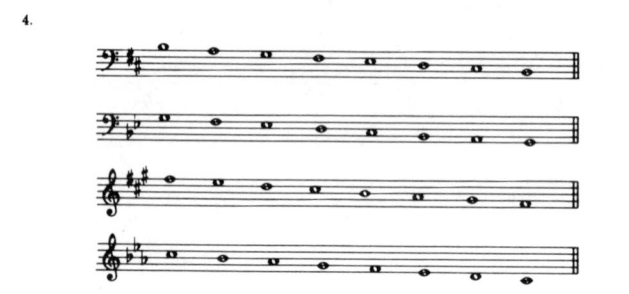

3.

4.

WORK SHEET 7 (p. 78)

1.

2. ascending melodic minor scale — raised sixth and seventh degrees
    minor triad — root, minor third, perfect fifth
    use the same key signature — relative major and minor
    major triad — root, major third, perfect fifth
    four semitones — major third
    descending melodic minor scale — lowered sixth and seventh degrees
    characteristic interval of minor scales and triads — minor third

3.

WORK SHEET 8 (p. 80)

JOSHUA FIT DE BATTLE OF JERICHO

British Navy Song

WORK SHEET 9 (p. 82)

1. a) MAJOR   d) MAJOR
   b) MAJOR   e) MINOR
   c) MINOR   f) MAJOR

2. SEVENTH DEGREE; RAISED:
   TO SUPPLY THE MAJOR THIRD FOR THE DOMINANT TRIAD

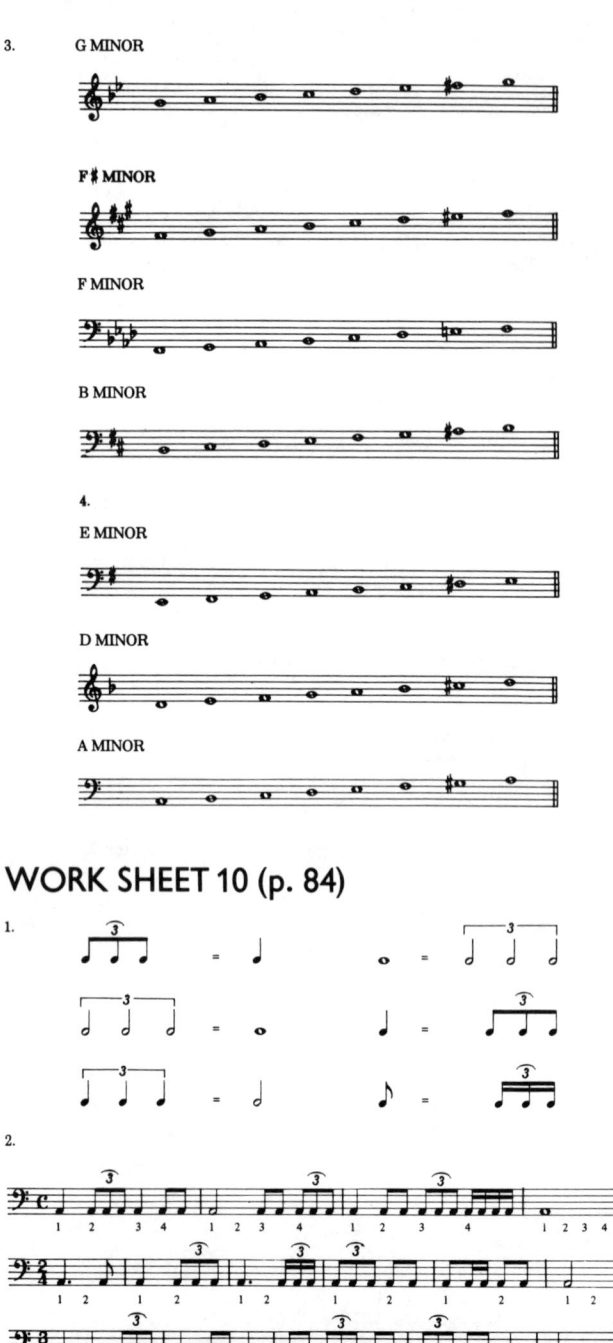

3.   G MINOR

   F# MINOR

   F MINOR

   B MINOR

4.
   E MINOR

   D MINOR

   A MINOR

WORK SHEET 10 (p. 84)

1.

2.

3.

F SHARP MINOR   E MAJOR   D MINOR   B MINOR   A FLAT MAJOR   C MINOR   A MAJOR   E MINOR

4.

5. a) PERFECT FIFTH   e) MINOR SECOND
   b) PERFECT OCTAVE   f) MAJOR SECOND
   c) MAJOR THIRD   g) SEVENTH
   d) MINOR THIRD

WORK SHEET 11 (p. 86)

1. a) SEVEN   g) EIGHT
   b) ELEVEN   h) FIVE
   c) THREE   i) TEN
   d) TWO   j) NONE
   e) TWELVE   k) NINE
   f) FOUR   l) ONE

2. a) PERFECT FOURTH   e) MAJOR SIXTH
   b) MINOR SEVENTH   f) PERFECT FIFTH
   c) MINOR THIRD   g) MINOR SIXTH
   d) MAJOR SEVENTH   h) MINOR SEVENTH

3.

MAJOR SECOND   MINOR SIXTH   PERFECT FIFTH   MINOR THIRD   MAJOR SEVENTH   PERFECT FOURTH   MINOR SECOND   PERFECT UNISON   MINOR SEVENTH

4.

WORK SHEET 12 (p. 88)

1.

2.

D7   B7   F7   E♭7   G7   C7

3.

[musical notation with chords: A7, G7, B7, F#7, D7, F7]

4.

D MINOR

[musical notation with V7]

B MINOR

[musical notation with V7]

5. D MAJOR A♭ MAJOR E MAJOR B♭ MAJOR A MAJOR F MAJOR
   B MINOR F MINOR C# MINOR G MINOR F# MINOR D MINOR

WORK SHEET 13 (p. 90)

1. a) G (major or minor)
   b) E♭
   c) A
   d) D
   e) E
   f) B♭

2.

[musical notation: D MAJOR, B♭ MAJOR, E MINOR, F MAJOR, C MINOR — each with V7 I]

3.

GERMAN FOLK SONG

[musical notation with chord symbols E♭, B♭7, E♭ — labeled I, V7, I]

[continuation with B♭7, E♭, B♭7, E♭ — V7, I, V7, I]

[continuation with Fm, B♭, E♭, B♭7, E♭ — ii, V, I, V7, I]

WORK SHEET 14 (p. 92)

1. FIRST, SECOND, THIRD, FOURTH, FIFTH, AND EIGHTH

2. MELODIC MINOR: G♯ A♯ (ascending) and A G (descending)
   HARMONIC MINOR: G A♯ (ascending and descending)

3.

4.

A HARMONIC MINOR

C♯ ASCENDING MELODIC MINOR

G MELODIC MINOR (Ascending and Descending)

F NATURAL MINOR

D HARMONIC MINOR

REVIEW WORK SHEET (p. 93)

1. THREE; MELODIC MINOR, HARMONIC MINOR, NATURAL MINOR; RAISED

2. a) B MINOR; C♯ MINOR; C MINOR; F♯ MINOR
   b) B♭ MAJOR; C MAJOR; A♭ MAJOR; G MAJOR; D♭ MAJOR
   c) G MINOR; D MAJOR; B♭ MINOR; F♯ MINOR

3.
B MINOR   C♯ MINOR   B♭ MAJOR   E MAJOR   G MINOR   A♭ MAJOR   F♯ MINOR

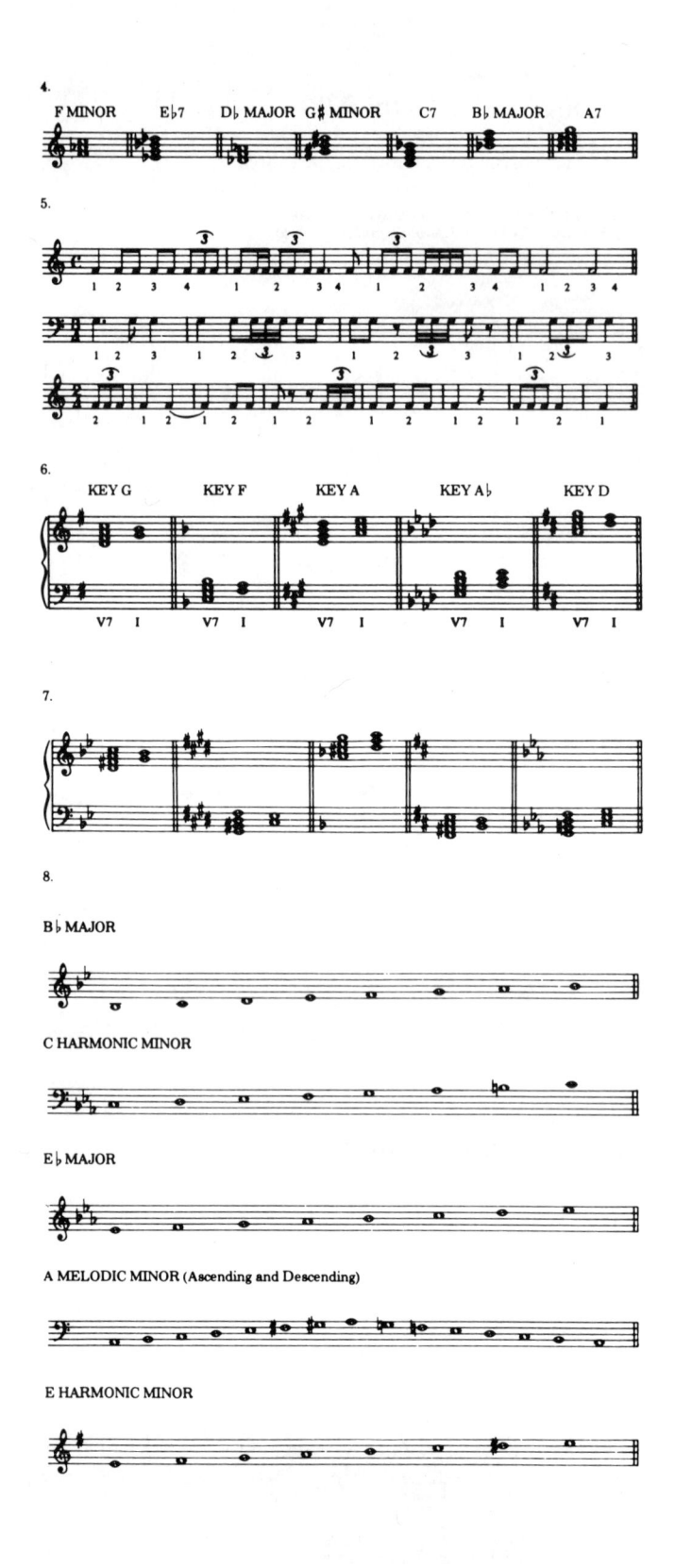

4.

F MINOR   E♭7   D♭ MAJOR   G♯ MINOR   C7   B♭ MAJOR   A7

5.

6.

KEY G   KEY F   KEY A   KEY A♭   KEY D

V7 I   V7 I   V7 I   V7 I   V7 I

7.

8.

B♭ MAJOR

C HARMONIC MINOR

E♭ MAJOR

A MELODIC MINOR (Ascending and Descending)

E HARMONIC MINOR